On Your Bike
Sussex

❋

Valerie Bennett

Photographs by James Bennett

COUNTRYSIDE BOOKS
NEWBURY, BERKSHIRE

COUNTRYSIDE BOOKS
3 Catherine Road
Newbury, Berkshire

To view our complete range of books,
please visit us at
www.countrysidebooks.co.uk

ISBN 1 85306 833 0

Designed by Graham Whiteman
Cover pictures supplied by Cleary Hughes Associates

Produced through MRM Associates Ltd., Reading
Printed in Italy

CONTENTS

Introduction   5

Guide to using this book   6

WEST SUSSEX ROUTES

1   Midhurst, Stedham Common and Selham   9
2   West Stoke, Emsworth, Bosham and Fishbourne   13
3   Hunston, the Centurion Way and Chichester   17
    Marina
4   Petworth, Northchapel and Kirdford   22
5   Coldwaltham, Bignor and Amberley   26
6   Arundel, Climping and Walberton   30
7   Southwater, Dial Post and the Downs Link   35
8   Henfield, Bramber and Fulking   39
9   Steyning and Shoreham   43
10 Hurstpierpoint, Clayton and Ditchling   48
11 Weir Wood Reservoir, West Hoathly and Horsted   52
    Keynes

EAST SUSSEX ROUTES

12 Ditchling Common, Sheffield Park and the Bluebell   56
    Railway
13 Forest Row, Groombridge and Ashdown Forest   61
14 Piltdown, Glynde and Isfield   66
15 Arlington Reservoir, Cuckmere Haven and   70
    Wilmington
16 Hailsham, the Cuckoo Trail and Pevensey   74
17 Bexhill, Pevensey and Herstmonceux   79
18 Robertsbridge, Bodiam and Battle   83
19 Hastings Country Park, Winchelsea and Pett   88
20 Camber, the Marsh Churches, Appledore and Rye   92

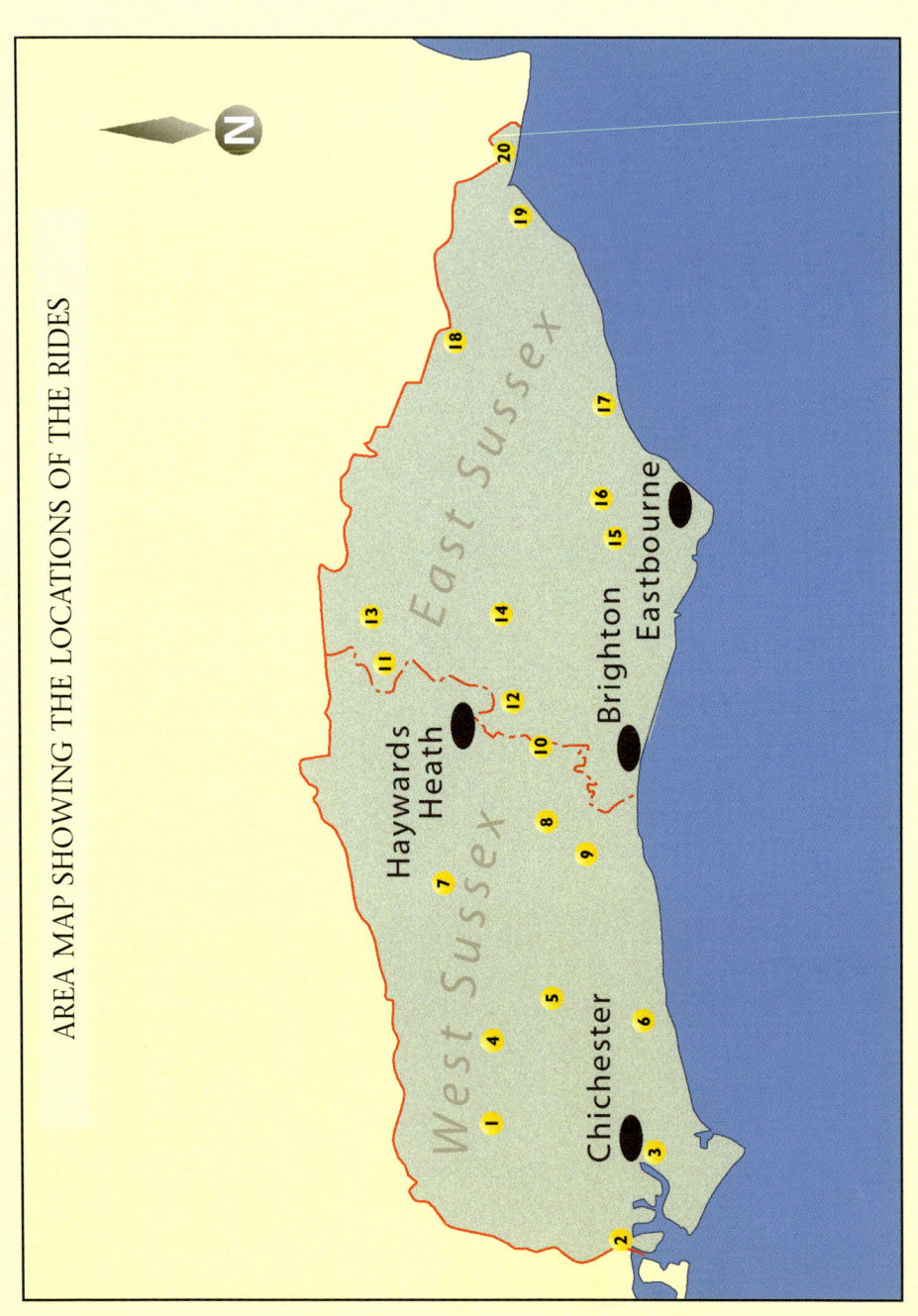

AREA MAP SHOWING THE LOCATIONS OF THE RIDES

INTRODUCTION

This book should help you to explore the natural beauty, geographic diversity and some of the colourful history that is to be found within the two counties of East and West Sussex. It is intended to encourage those new to cycling, those returning to it and the seasoned cyclist who wants to enjoy the countryside at a leisurely pace. You can cover ground quickly on a bicycle but you can also stop and look at whatever attracts your attention, be it an historic building, art gallery, a landscape or wildlife. The rides vary in length from 11¼ to 26 miles, with two mini rides around Arundel. Many of the rides lie geographically side by side so for those who wish to cycle further they can be linked easily with the help of a map, thereby making rides of up to 40 miles.

The aim has been to find circular routes using quiet roads and easy off-road routes, some from the National Cycle Network, parts of the South Coast Cycle Route and former railway tracks such as the Centurion Way, the Downs Link and the Cuckoo Trail. The quest for a minimum of steep hills was realised on some routes such as the coastal plain around Chichester, the Pevensey Marshes and over the county boundary into the marshes of Kent. However, the South Downs, Ashcombe Forest and the High Weald inevitably include undulations and occasionally steeper hills. These need give no cause for alarm as you can take your time and push your bike if necessary. There is plenty of spectacular scenery to admire as you do so and a change of pace can be a bonus.

The majority of bikes these days have at least 18 gears, which should enable you to cycle up most of the hills on these routes comfortably. Where there are off-road sections the lightweight sports variety is likely to be precluded, however. Don't dismiss riding a bike because of concerns about traffic. These routes are for the most part on quiet roads. There are only short stretches with traffic and these are clearly marked in the route description so that you can choose your route according to the experience of those with whom you are travelling.

Cycling offers the thrill of exploring new places and making your own discoveries on two wheels in the changing seasons. Have some wonderful days in the Sussex countryside.

Valerie Bennett

GUIDE TO USING THIS BOOK

Each route is preceded by details to help you:

The **number of miles** is the total number of miles that you will cover when using the core route. Some routes offer shorter or longer options for you to choose.

The **introduction** to the ride offers a broad picture of the places that you will pass and particular features that you may notice.

Although great care is taken to make route directions accurate and the directions are written to stand alone, nevertheless road lay-outs and cycle routes can change. The **use of a map** in conjunction with these routes is therefore highly recommended. Ordnance Survey Landranger (1: 50 000) should provide all the information that you need. OS Explorer maps (1:25 000) will offer even more detail. It is suggested that you take a map with you just in case it is needed or you wish to make a detour to visit an area of your choosing.

The grid reference of the suggested **starting point** is given but you may start from any convenient location on the route. Where a pub car park is suggested, the landlord has already given permission in principle for readers to park. However, all landlords ask that you telephone in advance or ask when parking in case the pub has a special function. They will appreciate it if you patronise their pubs, if only for a drink.

There is a leaflet called *Cycling by Train* available from the Cyclists Touring Club (telephone: 01483 417217). Telephone National Rail Enquiries 0845 7484950 for train times. Bikes are carried on a first come, first served basis on South Central Trains (telephone 0870 8306000) although there are many restrictions when using the London to Brighton service. The nearest **station**(s) is often on the route, but if not, use a map to reach the route from the station of your choice.

The names of pubs and tea rooms for **refreshment** are offered as a guide. Many of these have been sampled and enjoyed. However, it has not been possible to try every establishment and both landlords and menus change frequently so try other pubs or cafés that attract you as well. Remember that the laws relating to drinking and driving apply to cyclists as well and the Highway Code states that you must not ride under the influence of drink or drugs.

An indication is given regarding **the terrain**, whether it is undulating or reasonably level and whether sections of route are on or off-road. Warning is also given of any stretch of main road, or road with faster traffic, that needs to be negotiated. There are several routes that are relatively level such as those using the course of disused railway lines, the coastal plain and

those that run through marsh areas. Several rides are undulating and one or two have hills with more substantial climbs.

THE ROUTES

The rides are all **circular** so that you start and finish at the same place.

It is a good idea to read right through a route before setting out so that you are aware of what is involved. You can also plan so that you will have plenty of time for those places where you wish to linger. The directions have been written as clearly as possible. Instructions to change direction are written in bold type, ie: **turn R**. Sometimes the place name on a signpost is added to assist with directions.

You will find reference to NCN routes. This stands for **National Cycle Network.** It is one of the projects run by Sustrans, the charity that works on practical projects to encourage people to walk and cycle more to reduce motor traffic. Sections of these routes are used in this guide and referred to by NCN numbers so you can identify the appropriate route by the blue NCN signposts. Some proposed routes are still to be negotiated so cannot be included. Telephone Sustrans on 0117 929 0888, or the relevant Local Authority, to check the position. Quiet NCN routes will add to your enjoyment.

Suggestions are made for **shortening or extending** some rides. You can use a map to try alternatives yourself. Many rides lie very close to another so that you can find short road links to add two routes together, making rides of up to 40 miles in length.

At the end of each route there is more information about **places of interest**. These include notes about the architecture, history or people connected with the route. Most of the attractions are open at certain times from April to October each year. If you are particularly interested in visiting, telephone or check the internet for opening times to save disappointment.

SAFETY AND COMFORT

There are many common sense dos and don'ts. CTC, the national cyclists' organisation, offers a comprehensive *Get into Cycle Touring Basics* leaflet and also a specialised service for the leisure cyclist for everything you need from buying a bike to insurance (telephone 01483 417217 or www.ctc.org.uk).

Ensure that your bike is roadworthy and in particular that brakes and gears are in good working order and tyres are in good condition. Remember to take at least one pump, with the appropriate connector(s), for your bike and for those riding with you. Punctures should occur very infrequently if you avoid broken glass and walk around the thorns from recently cut hedges. As a precaution it is advisable to carry a spare inner tube just in case of a puncture and tyre levers to help remove the tyre.

If you cannot change an inner tube or mend a puncture it is worth getting someone to show you how before you set out. Alternatively have a strategy for dealing with the eventuality, such as taking a mobile phone with you for summoning assistance if necessary. Consider taking a bike lock in case you park your bike to explore an area.

Always be in control of your bike. Ride on the quietest of lanes as though a car is approaching. It may be. Make sure that pedestrians, on off-road routes and lanes, and horse riders are aware of your approach. Either fit your bike with a bell and ring it when necessary or call out to alert them of your approach.

Wear comfortable bright or light coloured clothing to ensure that you are seen. You are advised to wear shoes that will cope with mud where there are off-road routes. Even the best of unsurfaced off-road routes can have muddy patches after rain. Take a breathable waterproof jacket with you if there is likelihood of a shower. Make sure that you have no loose or dangling clothing that could get tangled in the wheel or chain. Use proper bike bags or panniers to carry things in.

Wearing a helmet is advisable and does offer some protection should you fall. There is plenty of literature available on the subject, from the Cyclists Touring Club among other sources.

Paul de Vivie, known as Vélocio, was born in 1853 and was considered to be the patron saint of cyclotourism. He is remembered for his seven commandments for the cyclist, for example: eat lightly and frequently, eat before you are hungry and drink before you are thirsty. So take plenty of water with you and carbohydrate foods such as bananas or biscuits.

Although not essential, a cycle computer is very useful for measuring distances and it will help you to see where you are on a map.

These are daytime rides but if there is any question of being out when dusk falls ensure that you have front and rear lights and a reflector.

Cycling offers a unique way of seeing some wonderful places. Enjoy your travels.

1

Midhurst, Stedham Common and Selham

17 or 21 miles

This ride starts in the lovely old market town of Midhurst and then describes an oval between the scarp of the South Downs and the River Rother. It offers a gentle exploration of delightful villages and the chance to enjoy a gallery of work by modern artists and craftsmen in South Ambersham. The route crosses Stedham Common Local Nature Reserve, where you may see woodlarks, lizards and the common blue butterfly in summer, southwards to the villages of Bepton and Cocking and on along the foot of the downs to Heyshott. Visit South Harting and National Trust owned Uppark (entrance fee) by following the alternative route, which is also a ride of 21 miles.

Map: OS Landranger 197 Chichester and The South Downs (GR 887218).

Starting point: The car park on the A272 by the Tourist Information Centre at Midhurst. There is also a car park on Iping Common, just off the A272 west of Midhurst.

By train: There is no railway line near the main route. If you are using the alternative route, however, South Harting is about 4 miles from Petersfield, which is on the main Portsmouth line.

Refreshments: In Midhurst there is a great variety of pubs and tea rooms. There is also the Royal Oak at Oaklands, the Blue Bell pub at Cocking, the Unicorn Inn at Heyshott, and the Three Moles at Selham. If you take the alternative route, South Harting has the White Hart and there is a National Trust restaurant at Uppark, when the property is open.

The route: Mainly along quiet undulating lanes apart from short sections in Midhurst town and the A286 where you can push your bike on the pavement. There are about 3 miles of off-road riding on the main route, along bridleways which are easy to negotiate in dry weather. **Alternative route** to South Harting and Uppark: Follow the main route past Stedham Common and continue down the hill to Elsted Marsh. **Turn R** to Dumpford. At T-junctions, **turn L** to Nyewood and **L** to South Harting. There is a detour to Uppark, high on the Downs, 1½ miles to the south with a good climb along the B2146. Return along the foot of the Downs via East Harting, Elsted and Treyford and join the main route at Didling. **Turn L** in Bepton and follow the road back to Midhurst (21 miles). **To shorten the route:** Follow the main route to the end of Pitsham Lane. **Turn L** into Bepton Road and ride to Bepton. Follow the main ride through Cocking and Heyshott to Midhurst (17 miles).

Turn L out of the car park into the A272 where you can push your bike on the pavement along the high street. Shortly **turn L** into Knockhundred Row. Notice the picturesque timber and sandstone buildings as you ride to Market Square and the celebrated Spread Eagle Hotel. Ride past the large pond and **turn L** into Selham Road, signposted to West Lavington. **Turn R** into Church Lane, signposted to Lavington church, and **R** again at the T-junction. The Royal Oak pub is about ½ mile on your right. Ride down the hill.

Turn L into the A286, or cross to walk on the pavement for about 200 yards. Pass the Greyhound pub and **turn R** into Pitsham Lane. Follow this bridleway between fields for just over a mile past Pitsham Farm and Dairy to meet Bepton Road. Cross over into another bridleway through woods. At a crossway with posts **bear R** with the bridleway up the rise (ignoring the footpath ahead). **Turn L** at the top and ride to Severals Road.

Turn R and cycle for ¾ mile to the A272. **Turn L** into the surfaced pathway alongside the road and follow it for ¼ mile. It veers away from the road to cross Woolmer Bridge. **Turn L** into a bridleway by a farm and soon **fork R** uphill. Cross a road into a bridleway across the heathland of Stedham Common for ½ mile to Elsted Road.

There is a car park opposite which offers an alternative to parking in Midhurst.

Turn L and cycle down the hill. **Turn L**, signposted to Didling, and ride along this tranquil lane past Old Pipers for about 1¾ miles to the hamlet of Didling. **Turn L** and ride for about 3 miles through the village of Bepton, with its sandstone and half-timbered cottages, to Cocking. Some of the cottages are owned by the Cowdray Estate and can be recognised by their yellow paintwork. You pass the Blue Bell pub. Moonlight Cottage, which serves coffees, light lunches and teas, is a short detour to your right on the A286.

Cross straight over the A286 and **bear R** down the lane beside the post office. Follow the lane as it passes the church. In 1¼ miles you reach Heyshott, the birthplace of Richard Cobden, leader of the Anti-Corn Law League. **Turn R** and the attractive Unicorn Inn is soon on your right.

Follow the road as it sweeps gently downwards for just under 1½ miles. **Turn R** at the crossroads. In less than a mile ride straight on by the stream, signposted to Selham (away from the major road). At a T-junction **turn L** towards Selham. In about 1¾ miles pass the Three Moles pub on your right and soon **turn L**, signposted to Midhurst.

Soon pass Selham church and in

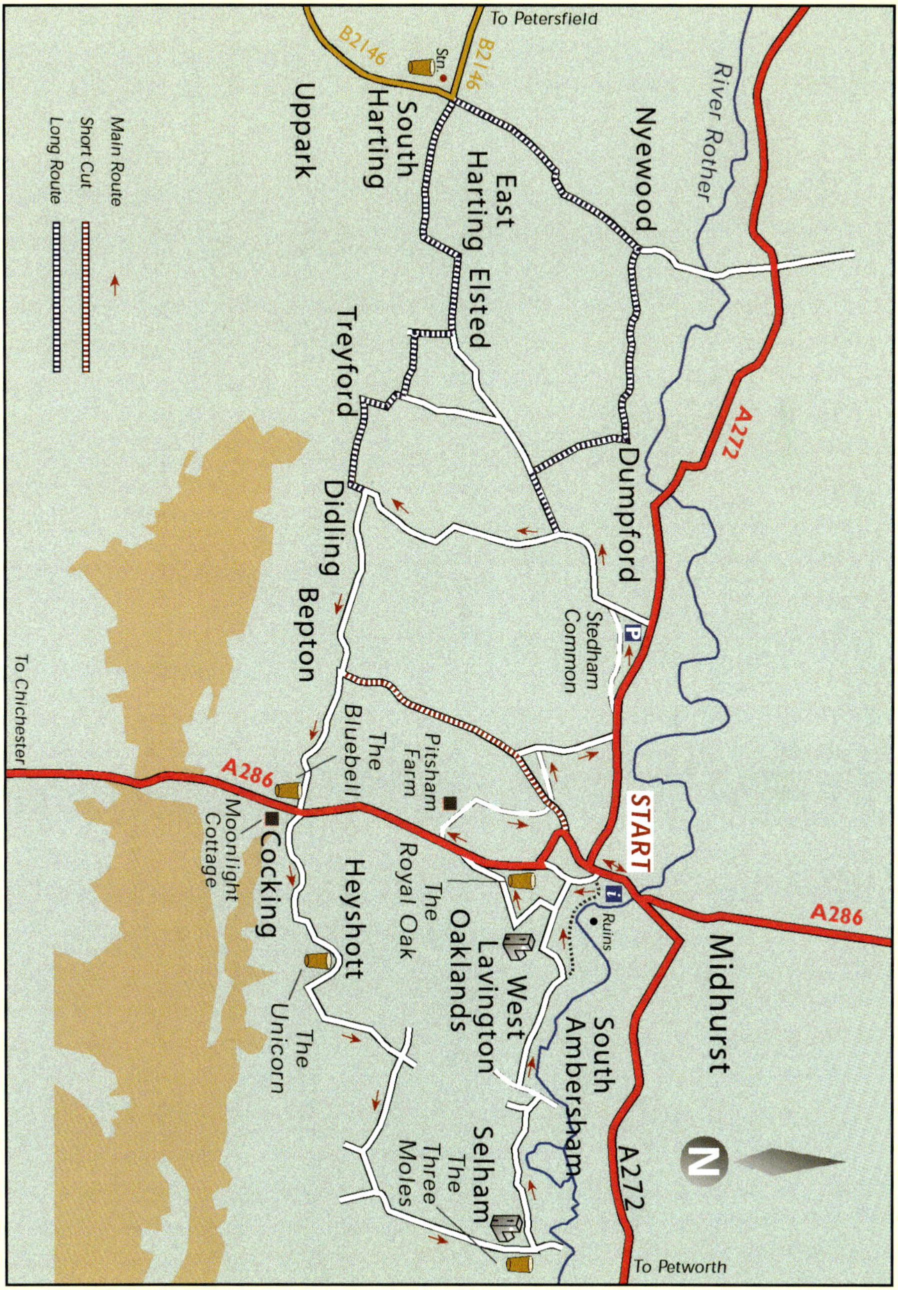

To Petersfield

To Chichester

To Petworth

River Rother

B2146

Stn.

South Harting

Uppark

East Harting

Elsted

Nyewood

Treyford

Didling

Bepton

Dumpford

Stedham Common

A272

Main Route
Short Cut
Long Route

The Bluebell

A286

Moonlight Cottage

Cocking

Heyshott

Pitsham Farm

The Royal Oak

The Unicorn

West Lavington

Oaklands

START

Ruins

South Ambersham

Midhurst

A286

A272

Selham

The Three Moles

N

The Spread Eagle Hotel, Midhurst

just over a mile **turn R** at the South Ambersham crossroads. **Bear L** just after the gallery and for 1¼ miles pass fields and stabling for polo ponies. Views of Cowdray House and Park open out to your right. At the bottom of the hill, as the road turns sharply left, continue ahead past Kennels Dairy. The bridleway narrows. **Turn L** immediately after crossing the bridge into the Wharf. **Turn R** towards Market Square and **R** again into the high street. The car park is shortly on your right.

• •

MIDHURST

This is an attractive old market town on the River Rother. Houses are clustered around the market square near the parish church where a curfew bell is rung each evening at 8 pm. It is said that a rider, lost in the dark, found Midhurst by following the sound of the church bell.

He bought a piece of land called Curfew Garden and gave it to the town in exchange for the nightly ringing of the bell. The ruins of Cowdray House, near the town car park, are the result of a fire in 1793. Legend has it that there is a Cowdray Curse and that this dates from the time that the first Viscount Montague of Cowdray decided to turn out the monks and live at Battle Abbey. The last monk to leave declared that the Montague line would perish by fire and by water. A week later the Viscount was drowned and two other members of the family drowned in 1815.

SELHAM AND SOUTH AMBERSHAM

The church of St James at Selham, dating back to Saxon times, has some fascinating wall paintings, a chancel arch with Scandinavian carving and some Victorian stained glass windows which are both unusual and beautiful. Further along the lane at South Ambersham there is a tiny art gallery that specialises in ceramic work but also has exhibitions of glass, jewellery, paintings and original sculpture. The gallery stands in a wild garden with a stream where you can wander. Telephone: 01798 861388 for opening hours or to request an appointment.

UPPARK AND SOUTH HARTING

There was a fire at Uppark in 1989 and many treasures were burnt or badly damaged but the 17th century house has now been restored. There are paintings, furniture, ceramics and a superb 18th century dolls' house to admire, also a peaceful garden. South Harting is the largest of the three Hartings, all of which nestle at the foot of the Downs. The village is able to claim at least three famous residents: Anthony Trollope, Gilbert White, the naturalist, and H.G. Wells, who spent some of his boyhood years at Uppark.

2

West Stoke, Emsworth, Bosham and Fishbourne

16 or 24 miles

Cycle along the foot of the South Downs from West Stoke to the village of Funtington and on to Emsworth, the harbour town just over the border into Hampshire. The route continues through the tiny village of Prinsted with its views of Thorney Channel where you can rest on a seat and look out over the salt marshes with their array of wildlife. Soon the way winds high above the A259 and the A27 to reach the attractive millpond in the village of West Ashling. Bosham, pronounced 'Bossum', is a gem. Try to leave time to enjoy the charms of its tidal creeks, views and beautiful church before you ride beside the water and on past the fields of the coastal plain to Fishbourne Roman Palace.

Map: OS Landranger 197 Chichester and The South Downs (GR 824088).

Starting point: The car park at West Stoke is just over 4 miles north-west of Chichester. From North Walls, Chichester, take the B2178 in the direction of Funtington. In about 3 miles you reach East Ashling. Turn right in the direction of West Stoke. In just over ¾ mile fork left, at a sharp right hand bend. The car park is shortly on your right.

By train: Bosham, Southbourne, Fishbourne and Emsworth stations are on the route.

Refreshments: The King's Arms, Flintstones Tea Room and the Sussex Brewery pub are in Emsworth. In Bosham there is the Mariners Coffee Shop, the Bosham Walk café, and the Anchor Bleu pub. The Black Boy pub is in Fishbourne and teas may be available at West Stoke church hall at certain times in summer.

The route: The major portion of the route has quiet lanes and is comparatively level. The B road near Funtington can have some faster traffic and there are some short stretches of busier roads around the Emsworth area.
To shorten the route: Turn L about ¾ mile after Funtington and **turn first L** again to pick up the main route near West Ashling. This shortens the route by about 8 miles and makes for a very quiet ride.
To extend the route: Detour to West Itchenor. In 1¾ miles from Bosham, Lower Hone Lane turns sharply left. A bridleway on the right leads to a spot where you can hail a water taxi to West Itchenor. For operating hours, telephone: 01243 775888. There is a proposed off-road NCN route from West Itchenor to Chichester Marina but it has yet to be negotiated. **Or:** Use a map to link the ride with route 3 to the east.

Make time to enjoy the charms of Bosham

Turn R out of the car park and cycle for 1½ miles to the T-junction at Funtington. **Turn R** into the B2146 through the village. Continue straight ahead and ride for 2 miles, signposted to Emsworth.

Soon after the MOD Research Establishment on your right, **turn L** into the B2147, signposted to Emsworth. Westbourne, an attractive village on the River Ems, is in about 1¼ miles.

Pass the church, go round a left hand bend and opposite the Wren Centre **turn L** into a cycle/pedestrian path. Ride ahead for ½ mile as the path leads into Westbourne Avenue.

Turn L into the B2147 and shortly L again into the B2148 past

Emsworth station. At the roundabout push your bike through the subway and shortly **turn R** into West Street. At the A259 go to the far side of the Millpond. The King's Arms is ahead on your right.

Turn L into Bath Road. The Millpond on your left is a beautiful area with swans. Dismount at the Promenade and enjoy views of Emsworth Channel as you push your bike along the footway between the pond and the harbour. On the far side is the Quay and Flintstones Tea Room, where you can sit outside and look across to the water.

Ride up South Street and **turn R** into the High Street. At the T-junction **turn R** into the A259. The Sussex Brewery pub is soon on your right.

The route now follows the blue South Coast Cycle Route as far as West Ashling. Shortly **turn R** into Thorney Road. In less than ½ mile **turn L** into Thornham Lane and in under ½ mile watch for the blue sign and **turn L** to ride along a way between fields to Nutbourne Marshes. This is inter-tidal mudland and a good place to picnic, particularly if the tide is in. Continue through the attractive village of Prinsted and **fork R.**

At the T-junction with the A259 at Southbourne **turn R** and shortly **turn L** at the mini-roundabout.

Short Cut

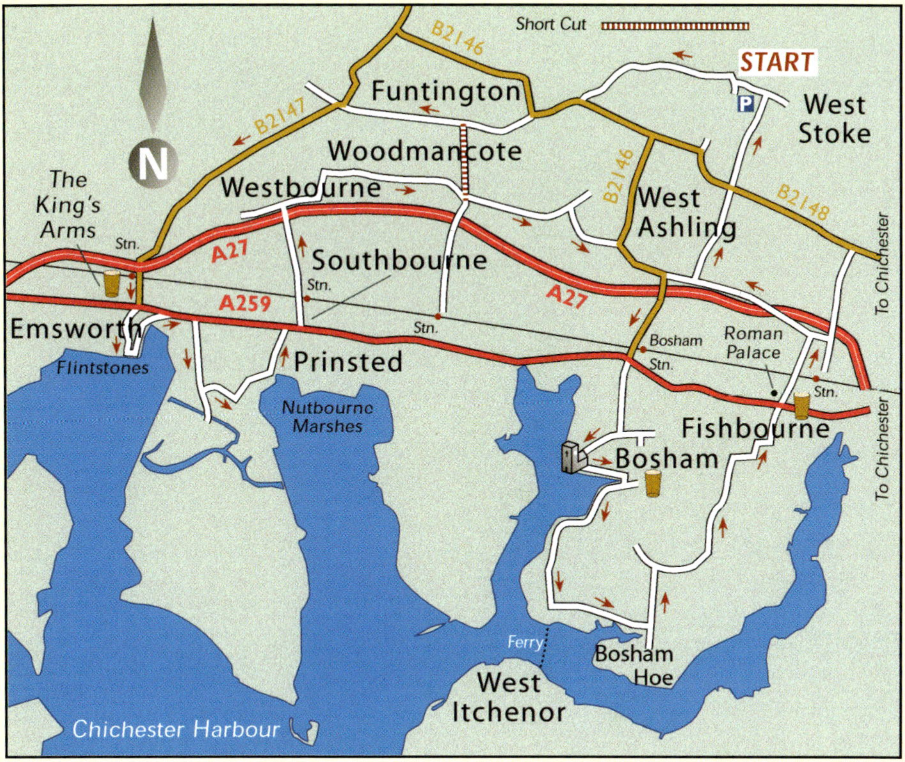

START

West Stoke

B2146

Funtington

B2147

Woodmancote

The King's Arms

N

Westbourne

Stn.

West Ashling

B2146

B2148

To Chichester

A27

Southbourne

Stn.

A27

Emsworth

A259

Stn.

Bosham Stn.

Roman Palace

Stn.

Flintstones

Prinsted

Nutbourne Marshes

To Chichester

Fishbourne

Bosham

Ferry

West Itchenor

Bosham Hoe

Chichester Harbour

Cycle over a bridge to cross the A27 and **turn R**. In ½ mile **bear R** toward Woodmancote. In 1½ miles at Cheeseman's Lane **turn L** and immediately **R**, signposted to West Ashling.

In about 1¼ miles you reach the attractive village of West Ashling with its pub and millpond. **Turn R** in the village onto the B2146 towards Bosham.

Cross the A27 and the spire of Chichester Cathedral comes into view. Cross straight over at the roundabout into Delling Lane.

In ½ mile **turn R** into Bosham Lane and ride on to the village, where you can wander and enjoy this lovely area. **Turn L** at the beach for a meander by the Bosham Channel with wonderful views across the water. If the tide is high there is a footpath where you may push your bike where necessary.

In about 3 miles from Bosham **turn R** at a pond by Lees Farm, signposted to Fishbourne, and follow Old Park Lane to the A259. This is an area where level fields meet the sky.

Turn R by the Black Boy into the

15

The attractive millpond at West Ashling

A259 and then **turn L** at the second turning, into Shorthill Lane (**turn R** for the Roman Palace). Go to the top of the lane, passing Fishbourne station, and **turn L** into Clay Lane. In ¾ mile cross above the A27.

Turn R in less than a mile into Mouthey Lane and keep straight ahead to West Stoke, crossing the B2178. **Turn L**, then **fork R** just past West Stoke House and the car park is on your right.

● ● ● ● ● ● ● ● ● ● ● ● ● ● ● ● ● ● ● ●

BOSHAM
Attractive cottages are built on a peninsula between two tidal creeks with the National Trust owned Quay Meadow offering an ideal position from which to gaze at boats and the sea. Legend has it that Canute lived in Bosham and his eight year old daughter is thought to have been buried in the church.

FISHBOURNE ROMAN PALACE
This is the largest Roman domestic building to be found north of the Alps and it houses one of the most extensive collections of mosaics in Northern Europe. It is thought to have been built around AD 75 and to have been the palace of a Celtic king. Remains of corridors, underfloor heating channels, a bath suite and other artefacts can be seen. Outdoors, a small Roman garden has been developed with replanting being carried out to its 1st century plan.

3

Hunston, the Centurion Way and Chichester Marina

20 or 25 miles

This route describes a circle around Chichester, visiting tiny villages, the Centurion Way, a prized cycleway with sculptures, and Chichester Marina with its myriad of boats. From the Gribble Inn in Oving with its very own brewery, ride across the former Battle of Britain airfield to Tangmere Military Aviation Museum and follow a bridleway past Goodwood Motor Racing Circuit. Consider pausing at Dell Quay for a drink whilst you admire the view and at Chichester Marina see a forest of masts. At Hunston there is a panoramic view of Chichester Cathedral across the meadows, as painted by Turner. There are two possible detours, one to the centre of Chichester along the canal towpath and a second to West Dean Gardens from East Lavant.

Map: OS Landranger 197 Chichester and The South Downs (GR 865023).

Starting point: Poyntz Bridge car park at Hunston. Take the B2145 from the Chichester bypass in the direction of Selsey. The car park is on the right just before you reach Hunston village.

By train: Chichester station is close to the northerly end of the Chichester Canal. Turn right out of the station, turn left and the canal is on your right. Take the canal path to Hunston and turn left onto the B2145 to join the start of the route.

Refreshments: Refreshment opportunities from pubs to snack kiosks and cafés abound so you are unlikely to go hungry or thirsty. The Gribble Inn at Oving is particularly inviting with its own brewery, log fire in season and attractive garden. Relax at the Crown and Anchor at Dell Quay whilst you admire the sights of the Chichester Channel, or cycle along the towpath from Hunston to Chichester where drinks and snacks are available at the small café at the end of the path. Alternatively there are many opportunities for tea in the city itself.

The route: The land is quite flat and at least half the route is easy off-road riding. The 1¼ mile bridleway beside the Goodwood circuit may need more negotiation in wet weather so use the alternative road route if necessary. The Harbour Authorities at Chichester Marina request that bikes are not taken across the footbridge on the lock. Park your bike and explore on foot, leaving the area by turning left before the marina. There are 2 or 3 miles of busier B roads around Hunston.

To extend the route: Turn L into the Centurion Way at Mid Lavant. Follow the blue signs for 2½ miles, to West Dean. At Binderton the Way runs alongside the road. **Turn R** into Church Lane at West Dean to visit the gardens (entrance fee) and church. **Or:** From Poyntz Bridge, Hunston, ride on the canal towpath to Chichester. **Or:** Use a map to link the ride with route 2.

Turn **L** out of the car park in the direction of Bognor, and follow the B2145 to the roundabout. Take the second exit into the B2166. Continue for just over 1 mile, crossing a second roundabout by the Walnut Tree pub. Soon **turn L** into Marsh Lane and wind along to the picturesque village of Merston with its Victorian estate cottages. **Fork R** and soon **turn R** into the A259 and ride on the cycle track for ½ mile.

Turn **L** in the direction of Colworth and soon **bear L** again. In 1 mile **turn L** and cycle to the far end of the village of Oving. **Turn R** into Gribble Lane and the inn is immediately on your right. Here you may decide to visit the brewery or to look out for the range of ales at the bar.

Follow Gribble Lane for just over ½ mile. **Turn L** into a bridleway, which leads across the disused airfield to Tangmere Military Aviation Museum. The museum (entrance fee) is well worth a visit and is packed with memorabilia.

Turn **R** from the museum and ride through the village and past the Bader Arms. **Turn L** into the cycle track beside the A27. Soon climb and cross over the bridge and **turn L** immediately. **Turn R** into the track signposted to Chichester. **Turn L** in ⅓ mile into the old Roman road, Stane Street. **Turn R** into Claypit Lane.

Either: Continue ahead for 1¼

Crossing the stream at the end of the Centurion Way

West Dean

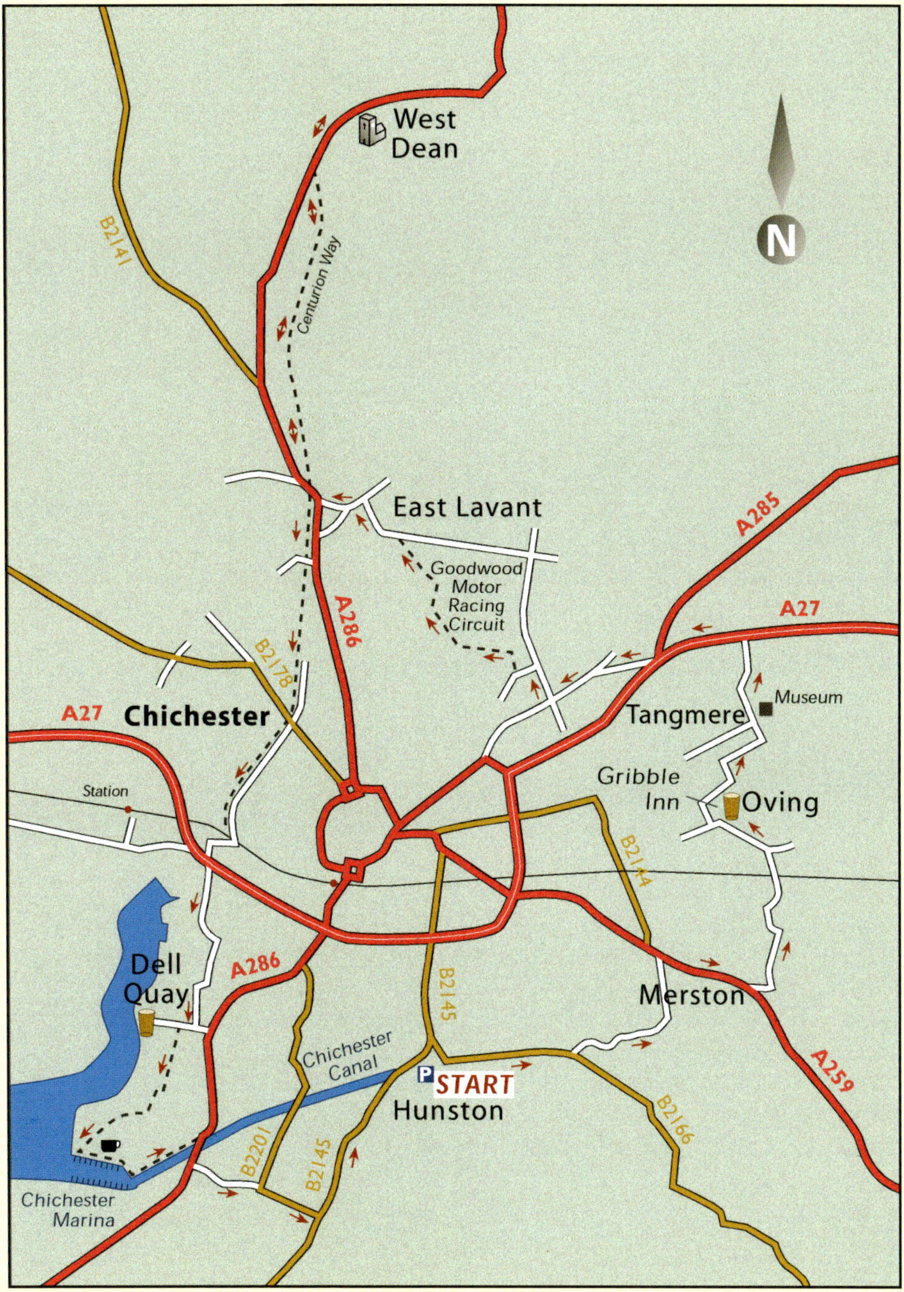

Centurion Way

B2141

East Lavant

A285

A27

Goodwood Motor Racing Circuit

A286

B2178

A27 **Chichester**

N

Tangmere

Museum

Gribble Inn

Oving

Station

B2144

Dell Quay

A286

Merston

A259

Chichester Canal

B2145

P **START**
Hunston

B2201

B2145

B2166

Chichester Marina

19

Pause to admire the view from Chichester Marina

miles and **turn L** into straight New Road.

Or: Turn L after the school and soon **turn R** into a bridleway which runs for about 1½ miles beside Goodwood Motor Racing Circuit. You may hear the scream of tyres on tarmac and later see planes flying low above your head as they prepare to land at Goodwood Aerodrome. There are occasional glimpses of the grandstand at Goodwood Race Course standing high on the Downs. **Turn L** at the T-junction.

Turn L in East Lavant village. Soon **turn R** at the green and climb the slope to the A286. Cross over into a narrow footpath and push your bike the short distance over the

bridge and **bear L** down to the Centurion Way.

To extend the ride to West Dean, along the section of the Centurion Way going northwards, follow the route in the box above.

Otherwise **turn R** and cycle about 2¾ miles along the Centurion Way towards Chichester. **Turn R** at the end of the Way, cross over the level crossing and soon **turn R,** signposted to Fishbourne. Use the cycleway under the A27, **turn L** on the cycleway, cross over and follow the off-road cycle track for a few yards. **Turn R** into Appledram Lane.

In 1¼ miles **turn R** at the T-junction. Perhaps detour to the

Crown and Anchor, ½ mile ahead, at Dell Quay by the Chichester Channel. A rest here offers a good view of the channel. Otherwise soon **turn L** into a farm road, signed as a footpath currently but it is a permissive cycleway.

Cycle along the farm track and **bear R** at the cottages, along a path beside fields. At Chichester Marina park your bike before the lock and perhaps explore this stunning area. You can sit on a seat and enjoy the view of the channel or watch boats entering or leaving the harbour through the lock.

Take an anti-clockwise route round the harbour and cycle 1¼ miles to the marina entrance (see the box above).

Turn R onto the A286, cross the bridge and **turn L** immediately. In ½ mile **fork R** into the B2201. Continue straight ahead, leaving the B road as it bends sharply right. **Turn L** at the T-junction into the B2145 and the car park at Hunston is just over a mile ahead on the left.

● ●

THE GRIBBLE INN BREWERY AT OVING

A complete small brewery is adjacent to the inn and a plaque on the wall offers interesting facts, figures and information. The brewery has the capacity to produce 4,320 pints of beer each week. Originally all taverns brewed their own beers to closely guarded recipes, which were passed down the generations. Tours are offered and these can be arranged at the inn.

TANGMERE MILITARY AVIATION MUSEUM

Many of the staff are former wartime RAF pilots, navigators and groundcrew. The museum is situated on the Battle of Britain airfield and lifesize models of planes such as the Hurricane and the Spitfire are on display. There is a special emphasis on the Royal Air Force at Tangmere and the battles over southern England during the Second World War. Information is available about the Lysander pilots who flew into occupied Europe with secret agents, as well as remains of aircraft and personal effects of those involved, both British and German. A cafeteria, picnic area and shop are all on site. Telephone: 01243 775223.

THE CENTURION WAY

Constructed on the old Chichester to Midhurst railway line, the Centurion Way offers a route through the countryside away from traffic for cyclists and walkers. Sculptures along the Way relate to local history and as the path crosses the course of a Roman road there is a centurion theme. Opened in 1881, the railway gradually declined until the rails were finally removed in 1993. The Local Authority and Sustrans combined with other organisations to create the path from Chichester to West Dean in the Downs. It is planned to extend it to the Open Air Museum at Singleton in due course.

4

Petworth, Northchapel and Kirdford

16 or 23 miles

From the country town of Petworth with its antique shops and magnificent house and park, this ride winds through the pastoral countryside and attractive villages of the Weald. Tranquil lanes lead to Northchapel just inside the Surrey border, where historic houses line the High Street. Cycle down the hill to Lurgashall village green at the foot of Black Down, the highest point in Sussex, and on to Upperton and Tillington with its unusual Scots Crown church tower. End the ride on a high note by entering Petworth Park at New Lodge West and cycling through the park by the imposing frontage of Petworth House.

Map: OS Landranger 197 Chichester and The South Downs (GR 977216).

Starting point: The free car park at Petworth. Turn left, leaving the one-way system just after the Star Inn. If this is full, try 'The Cut' to the east of Petworth. Take the A272 for about 3 miles in the direction of Wisborough Green. Watch carefully for crossroads, with Coldharbour signposted to the right. The car park is a short distance to the right and is on the route.

By train: Pulborough station is less than 3 miles from Fittleworth along the A283.

Refreshments: There are plenty of excellent places for refreshment, including the National Trust restaurant at Petworth House (no entrance fee for restaurant and shop). Just to the south of Petworth is Soames restaurant, and Fittleworth has the attractive Swan Hotel. Pubs on the route are the Half Moon and the Foresters Arms at Kirdford, the Deepwell Inn at Northchapel, the Noah's Ark at Lurgashall and the Horse Guards at Tillington. Tiffins Tea Room is in Petworth High Street.

The route: There are some distinctly hilly areas on the route but most hills are short, with just two or three longer climbs. The quiet lanes make for wonderful riding and there are lots of good downhill runs. There are short stretches of main road, the longest being a mile on the A283 at Fittleworth Hill. The off-road riding is on firm tracks and mowed grassland through Petworth Park.

To shorten the route by omitting Fittleworth: Turn into the one-way system at Petworth onto the A283 in the direction of Godalming. **Turn R** immediately after the junction with the A272 and **L** at Balls Cross and continue to Northchapel.

To extend the ride: Use a map to link with part of route 1.

Turn **R** out of the car park and **R** again along the High Street and into Grove Lane. Soames restaurant will shortly come into view on the right. Continue to the T-junction. **Turn L** in the direction of Fittleworth and continue for 2 miles as you join the A283 and then climb Fittleworth Hill. After a downhill run **turn L** in Fittleworth in the direction of Bedham. (Detour for refreshment at the Swan Hotel with its welcoming log fire in winter, a short distance off to the right. The village church is **R** and then **L**.)

In about ⅓ mile **fork R** along the narrow lane signposted to Bedham and climb the hill. In 1½ miles **bear R** to Wisborough Green and cycle for a further 1½ miles. Watch out for a notice 'Beware of low flying owls' before a good downhill run and a short climb. **Turn L**, signposted to Kirdford. There is a fine row of poplars to your right.

In ¾ mile you pass 'The Cut' on your left, the alternative car park.

Cross the A272 into the lane ahead. In less than a mile **turn R**, signposted to Kirdford, to reach the village, the church and the Half Moon pub in just over 1¼ miles. **Turn L** opposite the Kirdford village sign and pass the Foresters Arms. In just under a mile **turn R** into Scratchings Lane, signposted to Northchapel. Pedal for just over 2 miles to a T-junction and **turn R**.

Northchapel is about 2½ miles further on, at the end of Piper's Lane. On your way you will sight an Air Navigational Radio Beacon on a hill to the left. **Turn L** onto the A283 by the Deepwell Inn at Northchapel. In about ¼ mile, just past the village post office, **turn R**.

Ride for 1½ miles, passing Navant Hill where there are attractive cottages as you wind your way upwards. **Turn R** in the direction of Lurgashall (pronounced 'Lurgasale') and down the 10% hill into the village. The 16th century church once had Alfred, Lord Tennyson, as a member of its congregation. The Noah's Ark pub is also by the triangular village green.

Fork L just after the green. Continue for 1 mile to the T-junction and **turn R**. Ride the ups and downs for about 3¼ miles beside Petworth Park and cycle through the village of Upperton to Tillington, perhaps pausing at the cosy Horse Guards pub set above the road.

Turn L onto the A272 for about ⅓ mile and **turn L** through the gate at New Lodge West, an entrance to Petworth Park. Follow the track and **bear R** at the lake to cycle beside it towards Petworth House. At the end of the lake **turn L** off the track and cycle on the broad grass way towards the wrought iron gate to the left of the house. Go through the gate and under the bridge and **bear R**. For entry to the house follow the signs.

To Godalming

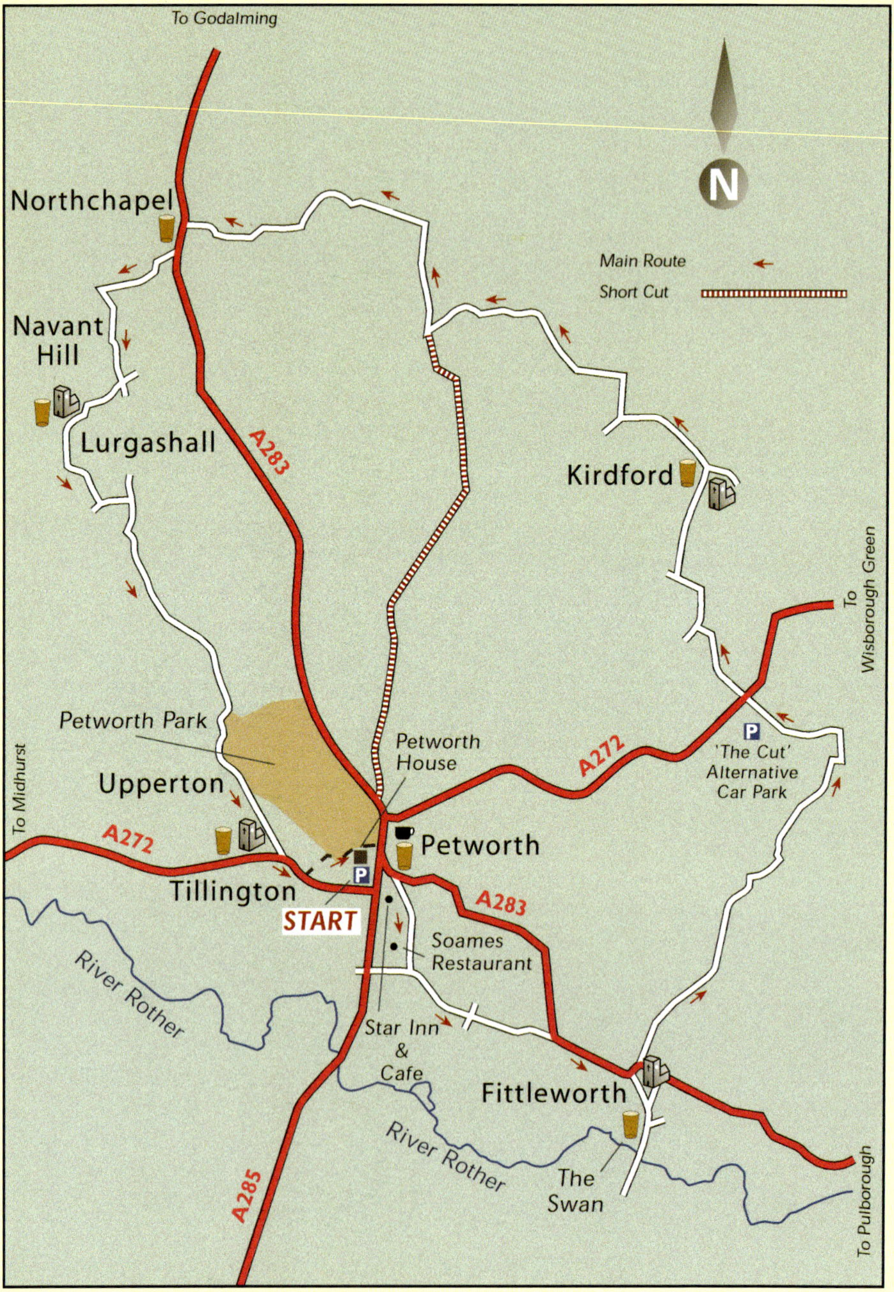

N

Northchapel

Main Route
Short Cut

Navant
Hill

Lurgashall

A283

Kirdford

To Wisborough Green

Petworth Park

Petworth
House

A272

'The Cut'
Alternative
Car Park

To Midhurst

Upperton

A272

Petworth

Tillington

START

A283

Soames
Restaurant

River Rother

Star Inn
&
Cafe

Fittleworth

River Rother

The
Swan

A285

To Pulborough

Pretty cottages in Kirdford

Turn R into the A283 and follow the one-way system into the centre of Petworth. **Turn L** after the Star Inn to reach the car park.

• •

KIRDFORD

The history of Kirdford has strong connections with the glass industry, and local glass features in the village sign, erected to commemorate the coronation of King George VI. There is an unusual plaque on the vicarage wall headed 'Degradation of Drunkeness'. Well worth reading, but for the cyclist it may have the effect of making you feel that today's lunchtime drinking should be moderate as drunkenness is said to fill the legs with water.

TILLINGTON

This attractive estate village stands just up from the main Petworth to Midhurst road on a sandstone ridge above the River Rother. On the top of the church tower of All Hallows is Britain's most southerly Scots Crown spire, which is formed by flying buttresses. Built in 1807 it is thought that the Scots Crown was intended to offer a notable entrance for the western approach to the Petworth Estate. Just across the road the Horse Guards pub is so named as that regiment had been billeted in Petworth Park during the Napoleonic Wars.

PETWORTH PARK

The 17th century Petworth House has a fine collection of paintings with works by Turner, Van Dyke and Reynolds, to name but a few. The beautiful 700 acre park, landscaped by Capability Brown, has a large lake and fallow deer herd which is reputed to be the largest in England. Cycling is allowed in the park, where there are some wonderful views of the surrounding countryside.

Coldwaltham, Bignor and Amberley

13½ or 17 miles

This route enables you to travel by bicycle through some of the most picturesque villages and diverse countryside that West Sussex has to offer. You ride through the four delightful villages of Sutton, West Burton, Bury and Amberley with their thatched and mellow stone-built houses and pass the Roman Villa at Bignor. The countryside is at first wooded and then opens out, offering wide downland views up to Bury Hill. Rest at the White Horse at Sutton or perhaps at the Sportsman pub at Amberley where you can look out across the Wild Brooks. You may also enjoy browsing in the Amberley Pottery. The extended route takes you to the wonderful Parham House (entrance fee).

Map: OS Landranger 197 Chichester and The South Downs (GR 031163).

Starting point: The car park at Coldwaltham to the south-west of Pulborough. Coldwaltham is on the A29, just over 2 miles south of the mini-roundabout at Pulborough. Turn off to the south-east at the crossroads and the car park is on your right just before the bridge over the River Arun.

By train: Amberley station is ½ mile from the route. Follow the B2139 in the direction of Storrington for ½ mile and then join the route to Amberley.

Refreshments: The Swan Hotel (½ mile from the route) at Lower Fittleworth, the White Horse at Sutton, Bignor Roman Villa, the Squire and Horse at Bury and the Black Horse and the Sportsman at Amberley.

The route: In general it is a fairly quiet and easy ride although there are some undulations. Near Amberley there is less than a mile off-road on a part of the South Downs Way. The extension to Parham includes a mile along the A283 where there can be fast traffic.

To extend the route: Visit Parham by turning off the main route north of Rackham and cycling along the A283 and then through the grounds to the house when open. **Or:** Use a map to link the ride with route 4.

Turn **L** out of the car park and ride to the T-junction with the A29. Cross straight over and cycle through woods and past fields for a mile. **Turn R** at the T-junction into Tripp Hill. Either **turn L** in less than ½ mile at Coates Lane or detour for ½ mile to visit Fittleworth and the excellent Swan Hotel.

The River Arun near Bury is a good place for a picnic

Continue along Coates Lane for about 1¾ miles and **turn L** at a crossroads. Soon **bear R** to Crouch Farm and Barlavington. **Turn L** at the T-junction and **turn L** to see the hamlet of Barlavington. Return to Folly Lane and follow this for a mile. **Turn L** at New Barn into the village of Sutton.

Bear R down the hill and up a short sharp one to Bignor church on your left. Continue ahead, **bearing R** past cottages and on to the Roman Villa. Ride for a mile to the attractive village of West Burton and then on to the T-junction.

Turn R into the A29 for a few yards towards the Squire and Horse pub. **Turn L** along the lane by the pub in the direction of Bury and soon **R** into Houghton Lane (unless you wish to continue ahead for a short detour to Bury village with its church and access to the River Arun, where you can sit on a seat and picnic).

Continue along Houghton Lane and in a mile **turn L** along the South Downs Way. Here there are expansive views across the Wild Brooks and up to Bury Hill. Cross the river by the iron bridge, **turn R** and shortly **bear L**, following the track as it winds to the left and then right across the railway line. **Turn L** onto the B2139 and in less than ½ mile **turn L** towards Amberley. The village is a delight and well worth exploring. To your left is the church and pottery where you can browse.

Cycle up the hill past the Black Horse pub. **Bear R** in the direction of Rackham, passing the Sportsman pub on your left. About a mile from the Sportsman **turn L** at the T-junction and ride along the lane beside the Parham grounds.

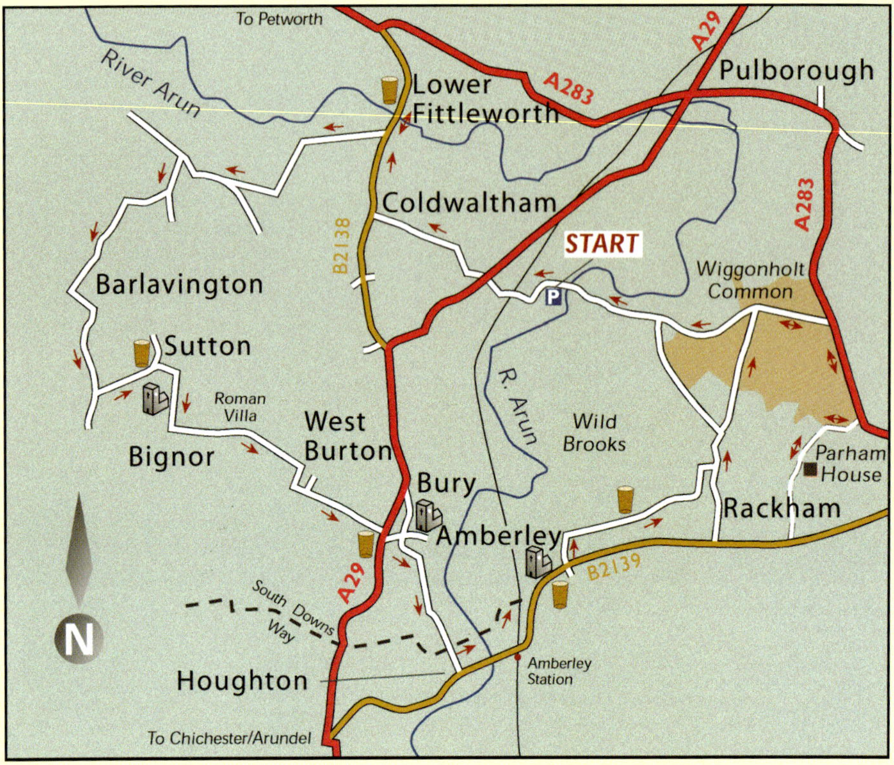

Either: Continue ahead to Wiggonholt Common if you are going to visit Parham, passing a footpath into the grounds. **Turn R** at the T-junction and then **R** again along the A283 for a mile. The drive (¾ mile) to Parham House is on your right. After visiting the house, retrace your way along the A283 for a mile. **Turn L** and

continue for 3 miles. You will cross Wiggonholt Common and just after Greatham Bridge the car park is on your left.

Or: Turn L to Greatham Common and **L** again at the T-junction, riding for 2 miles through wooded country, past fields and over the River Arun back to the car park.

● ● ● ● ● ● ● ● ● ● ● ● ● ● ● ● ● ●

BIGNOR AND THE ROMAN VILLA

Bignor village is on the line of Roman Stane Street. A complete excavation in the 1920s found the site, which covers four acres and contains one of the finest examples of Roman architecture in this part of England. The mosaics are of

Thatched cottages line the road in Amberley

particularly fine quality and are on display. Telephone: 01798 869259 for opening times.

AMBERLEY

The village has been called 'the pearl of Sussex'. There are not only picturesque thatched cottages, wisteria-hung mellow stone houses and a church but also a castle which is now a hotel. St Michael's church dates from the 12th century and has red ochre wall paintings. Amberley is sited at the foot of the Downs and by the Wild Brooks, a nature reserve of watercourses and meadows that become flooded in winter. The beauty of the village may have given rise to envy in the past as the villagers were known as the Amberley yellow-bellies. They had to dig peat from the brooks for heating and the women were said to lift their skirts to warm themselves over smoky fires. They were also said to be born with webbed feet because of the winter flooding. The Chalk Pits Museum, where there are working exhibits of industry in Sussex

through the ages, is on the site of an old lime-burning quarry near the station.

PARHAM HOUSE

Parham, now a family home, is a beautiful Elizabethan mansion in 875 acres of ancient parkland with a herd of fallow deer. It has a long history, having been owned originally by the monastery of Westminster before the dissolution of the monasteries. It is said to be one of the best Elizabethan houses in Sussex, and has some fine paintings, tapestries, rare needlework and china. The house, gardens and maze are open to the public. Listen for the resident ghost at Parham, which is said to be heard but never seen. In the 19th century the small church that stands nearby was virtually rebuilt but retains box pews and a squire's pew with its own fireplace. The rector was said to know when his sermon was too long as the squire began to shovel the coal noisily onto the fire. For Parham's opening times, telephone: 01903 744888.

29

Arundel, Climping and Walberton

15 miles with optional additions of 2½ and 7 miles

Arundel is a historic town with one of the best preserved castles in the country, so try to leave yourself time to wander and perhaps explore the castle and the cathedral. You may wish to browse later in the antique shops or speciality sports shops that you pass on the outward ride. To avoid the busy A27 you can take take the adventurous bridleway through ancient woodland in Binsted Wood. You ride to Climping and Atherington with its unspoilt coastline and sand-dunes, you can sample the good food at the Black Horse pub, explore a restored windmill with its own teashop at Barnham and enjoy the flowers of Walberton in summer. Detours to attractive Burpham, a village in the Downs, and to Offham by the River Arun are options and can stand as rides in their own right.

Map: OS Landranger 197 Chichester and The South Downs (GR 021071).

Starting point: The car park in Arundel at the bottom of the town by the river. There is a charge. Alternatively you can park by the roadside on the way to Offham. Beyond the bridge there are convenient laybys.

By train: Arundel, Ford and Barnham stations are on the route.

Refreshments: On these rides you are spoilt for choice and some establishments are open all day in the summer months. There are the Black Horse and the Oyster Catcher at Climping, the teashop at Barnham Windmill, the Holly Tree at Walberton and the Black Horse at Binsted. In Arundel there is great variety. On the Offham section there is the Black Rabbit by the Arun, and Burpham has the George and Dragon.

The route: There are some lovely places on this route but it is a more adventurous ride with faster traffic on the straight road from Arundel to Climping. The byway to Climping Beach is easy whilst the 1½ mile bridleway through Binsted Wood is more of a challenge and best used in drier weather conditions with *a hardy bike*, unless you get off and push. There is a footpath of ½ mile after the bridleway where you should also push your bike.

To extend the route: The detour to Offham (2½ miles total) is flat and easy. Or: Detour 7 miles to Burpham. There are a few yards on the A27 and then ups and downs along a quiet lane.

From the car park **turn L** and ride across the mini-roundabout to follow the High Street up the hill. **Turn L** opposite the Norfolk Arms into Tarrant Street with its antique and sports shops and cafés. **Turn L** at the T-junction and go to the roundabout and onto the A27. Take the second exit – in the direction of Ford.

In ¾ mile **turn R** into Priory Road. As you climb, cast a glance over your right shoulder for a view of Arundel. **Bear L** at the junction, signposted to Tortington, and sweep down the hill with views across the fields to Tortington Manor.

Turn R at the T-junction and cycle for 2 miles. You pass Ford station, a model of a Hawker Hunter at the former Ford Airfield, and Ford Open Prison. St Mary's church, Climping, just by the prison, is said to be one of the best medieval village churches in the country. The whereabouts of the key can be found on the noticeboard in the porch.

At the roundabout take the second exit, ahead. In a few yards **turn R** and ride past Climping School. **Bear L** into the byway for less than a mile. At the T-junction the byway becomes a footpath so push your bike to the car park for access to the beach with its extensive sand-dunes and good swimming.

Ride up Climping Street and perhaps rest at the Black Horse pub. Afterwards pass flint cottages and a blacksmith's forge. **Turn L**

Arundel Castle is worth exploring

and immediately **R** at the T-junction into the B2233. The enticing thatched Oyster Catcher pub is on your left. Continue for 2½ miles through Yapton and on to Barnham Windmill, where you may decide to view the mill.

Continue for a further ½ mile and ride under the railway bridge at Barnham. **Turn R** immediately after the bridge and follow the road into the village of Walberton, where flowers predominate in summer. The Holly Tree pub offers fresh Selsey crab on occasions. At the roundabout **turn L** and in ½ mile **turn R**, signposted to Binsted.

Ride down the hill and **turn L** at the T-junction unless you wish to visit the Black Horse pub, a few yards to your right. In about ¼ mile **turn R** into a bridleway. At first it passes fields then it runs through ancient woodland. Continue for 1½ miles and **turn L** into a lane.

Soon **turn R**, then, pushing your bike, **turn L** into a footpath and follow it for ½ mile. Emerge in a housing estate and, keeping a fence to your left and then a hedge to your right, go to the road. **Turn R** and then **L** into Canada Road. There is a good downhill run to the T-junction. **Turn L** to the

The historic town of Arundel

roundabout on the A27.

Take the third exit to Arundel. If you wish to visit the cathedral **turn L** into Parsons Street. Otherwise follow the road, moving to the right hand lane as the road divides. The entrance to the castle is on your left. Continue down the hill to the mini-roundabout.

Either: Return to the car park.

Or: Make a short detour to Offham. With the car park to your right cycle 1¼ miles along Mill Road to the Black Rabbit pub, where you can sit on the terrace and relax by the meandering River Arun. Retrace your route towards Arundel and consider a visit to the Wildfowl and Wetlands Centre (entrance charge), where you can see thousands of birds and migrant wildfowl in a variety of habitats.

Or: For the 7 mile detour to the idyllic downland villages of Wepham and Burpham, go to the mini-roundabout and ride over the bridge. **Turn L** and at the large roundabout take the first exit into the A27. **Turn L** immediately after the bridge and soon there are outstanding views of the castle and cathedral to your left.

Follow the undulations of the lane for 2½ miles through the pretty village of Wepham and past the thatched cottages in Burpham to the cosy George and Dragon pub. Retrace the route through Wepham and past Arundel station to the large roundabout, where you take the second exit back to the centre of Arundel.

Burpham

ARUNDEL

Arundel has a unique skyline made up of the castle, the Roman Catholic cathedral and the parish church of St Nicholas. Standing on a hilltop above the Arun valley, Arundel was always considered to be of strategic importance and a motte and bailey was built by the Normans on the site of the present castle. The castle has been the family seat of the Dukes of Norfolk for more that 400 years but was rebuilt at the end of the 19th century. The architect of the Roman Catholic Cathedral of Our Lady and St Philip Howard was Joseph Hansom, inventor of the Hansom cab. If you are here at Corpus Christi (May or June) visit the cathedral to see the carpet of flowers, a tradition taken from the village of Sutri outside Rome. Information about the castle and the Wildfowl and Wetlands Centre and details of opening times can be obtained from the Tourist Information Centre in the High Street.

BARNHAM WINDMILL

The mill, built in 1829 by the millwright Henry Martin, was built to replace the post mill blown down two years earlier. It is being restored to working order to enable wheat to be ground both for demonstrations and for sale. Visitors may climb the mill stairs, view the restoration work and see the pictorial story of the work that has been undertaken – as well as sampling the teashop.

BURPHAM

Burpham and neighbouring Wepham are attractive downland villages. In medieval times there was a leper settlement within walking distance of the Norman church of St Mary. Blessings could be dispensed to the victims by the priest from the special window. Much later, the Rev Edward Tickner Edwardes, vicar of Burpham from 1927 to 1935, claimed fame by becoming a well known writer of novels, local history, folklore and, unusually, material concerning honeybees.

7

Southwater, Dial Post and the Downs Link

21 miles

The route is particularly quiet and there are long off-road stretches as it threads its way along the Downs Link and around country lanes where there is little traffic. The way passes the playing fields of Christ's Hospital School and you can visit the beautiful 12th century Itchingfield church and Shipley Windmill if you should pass when the latter is open. Ride through the hamlet of Dragons Green with its aptly named pub and on to the little village of Dial Post. Pause for tea under an umbrella at the attractive Barn Nursery restaurant and then on along farm roads through pastoral Lock Estate to Partridge Green. Cycle back along the green wildlife corridor of the Downs Link. Train enthusiasts will enjoy the old railway carriage full of information at West Grinstead, staffed by volunteers.

Map: OS Landranger 198 Brighton and Lewes (GR 162263).

Starting point: The car park at Southwater Country Park. Turn off the A24 Horsham–Worthing road at the roundabout to the south of the Southwater bypass. Follow the brown signs to Southwater Country Park. Turn first right and follow Cripplegate Lane. Turn left into the Country Park where signed. The main car park is then to your right.

By train: Christ's Hospital station is less than ½ mile from the route. Ride in the direction of the school, fork right to the bridge and join the route.

Refreshments: There are some very good and attractive pubs on this route. The Bax Castle is near the start by the Downs Link, the Queen's Head is at Barns Green, and the aptly named George and Dragon is at Dragons Green. The Countryman at Shipley is just south of the route. When Shipley Windmill is open, teas are available in Andrew Hall (the village hall). A relaxing break can be taken at the Barn Nursery restaurant at Dial Post, where a good variety of food and drink is available all day. The Crown is also at Dial Post and the Partridge is just to the right of the Downs Link at Partridge Green.

The route: There are one or two short climbs but in general it is a particularly easy, quiet and fairly flat ride. You have to cross the A24 dual carriageway near Dial Post but there is a central reservation. The Lock Estate and the Downs Link provide off-road riding away from traffic. There are some stony sections on each but they are easy to negotiate. There are likely to be mud patches on the Downs Link in wet weather.

Climb up the short slope from the main car park and **turn R** into the Downs Link. Follow the Link signs and ride along the former platform of old Southwater station. After crossing a field and passing through a gate you will see the Bax Castle pub on your right. Follow the course of the old railway track for a further ¾ mile and then follow the driveway beside Christ's Hospital playing fields. Shortly, still following the Downs Link, go ahead, away from the driveway, into a narrow path. **Turn L** by the entrance drive to the school and **L** again to cycle over the railway bridge and down the hill to the T-junction.

Sailing on the lake at Southwater Country Park

Turn L in the direction of Barns Green and soon **turn R**. In ¼ mile it is worth making a short detour. Cycle round the right hand corner to 12th century Itchingfield church with its 10 foot wide Priest's House in the churchyard and enormous ancient yew trees. Return to the corner by Itchingfield School and ride ahead into the bridleway, which runs over a private driveway. This winds through woods for a mile, through the lodge gate and past the rear of Muntham House School and farm buildings. Watch for speed ramps near the end of the drive before passing Barns Green village hall and green.

Turn R at the T-junction and soon the Queen's Head is on your left. In about ¼ mile go ahead over the level crossing, signposted to Brooks Green, into Emms Lane. There is a short climb and then a downward run to a T-junction. **Turn L** and immediately **R** signposted to Dragons Green.

In ½ mile **turn R** at a grassy triangle by a house and **R** again at the T-junction. In less than a mile **turn R** by the George and Dragon pub. Cross the A272 into the lane ahead. Soon **turn L**, signposted to Shipley, and Shipley Windmill is in about ¼ mile. Watch for the sign indicating the windmill and **turn R** into a driveway to visit. If it is open then teas should be available in the village hall. Follow the lane through Shipley as it winds sharply left and right and **turn R** at a T-junction. Cycle for 2 miles past the village of Dial Post and the Crown Inn to the A24.

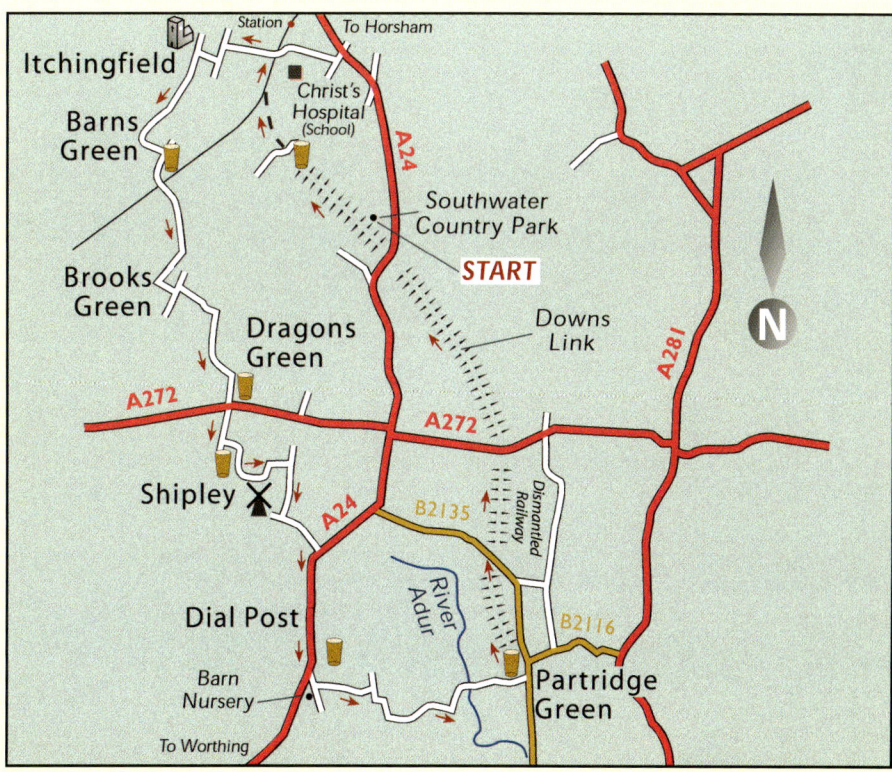

Cross with care straight over the dual carriageway into Honeybridge Lane. You may decide to browse, or to stop for refreshment, at the Barn Nursery. Immediately opposite the 'deliveries' entrance, **turn L** into a driveway and cling to the bridleway, following the bridleway signs, as it weaves for about 3 miles (avoid the various footpaths leading off).

In detail: follow the track to a T-junction. **Turn R** and follow the, now surfaced, driveway downwards for ½ mile. **Bear L** and views open out to the Downs in the distance. At Lock Farm the bridleway takes an anti-clockwise route around the farm cottages and buildings and narrows to a pathway between attractive houses. It finally runs to the right into the farm estate road and crosses the River Adur. At the T-junction **turn L** onto the B2135 for just a few yards.

At the bridge, **turn L** almost immediately to rejoin the Downs Link. The route now lies straight ahead for about 5 miles back to Southwater Country Park. The Link shortly passes close to Partridge Green and should you wish to visit the Partridge pub there is a short track to the right. Pass over and under two bridges and past the old

King's Mill at Shipley is Sussex's youngest mill

DOWNS LINK

The bridleway was established to link the North Downs Way and South Downs Way national trails. The trail crosses the Low Weald and follows two former railway lines for about 38 miles. One was from Guildford to Christ's Hospital and the other from Itchingfield Junction, near Christ's Hospital, to Shoreham-by-Sea. Both railways were closed in 1966 as a result of the Beeching cuts.

SHIPLEY WINDMILL

You may possibly recognise this as it was filmed as the fictional home of Jonathan Creek, the television super sleuth. King's Mill is the largest, the tallest and the youngest in Sussex. It is built on a brick base, two storeys high and is an eight-sided smock mill, so named as it is supposed to look like an ancient farm labourer's smock. Erected in 1879 it was later bought by Hilaire Belloc, who is reputed to have had a habit of doffing his large black hat to the mill upon his return from his travels. The mill was closed in 1926 as Belloc is said to have found that the mill traffic passing his study window distracted him from writing. It is now owned by a charitable trust and works when volunteers are available and the wind permits. Telephone: 01403 730439 for opening hours and further information.

West Grinstead station. Here there is an original railway carriage with interesting models, leaflets and information for the railway enthusiast.

In 1 mile cycle under the A272 and in a further 1¾ miles cross the Copsale Road. The Country Park is less than 1 mile ahead.

Henfield, Bramber and Fulking

18 miles

Cycle from Henfield to Bramber along the Downs Link to enjoy some off-road riding on one of the more scenic sections above the water meadows. At Bramber consider a climb to the ruins of the Norman castle high above the village and perhaps visit the fine timbered St Mary's House. The river valley then gives way to a rolling lane along the base of the Downs with views across the Weald. In Fulking, where there is a long history of sheep rearing, pause at the Shepherd and Dog and then find, close by, the village fountain where the sheep washing used to be carried out. The return ride is along shady lanes, through Blackstone and then a fast and fairly flat route to reach Henfield.

Map: OS Landranger 198 Brighton and Lewes (GR 204163).

Starting point: The car park at Henfield. The village lies on the A281 south of Horsham. Turn off westwards into Church Street and continue into Upper Station Road. The car park is on the right hand side just past the Old Railway Tavern.

By train: There is no station on, or close to, the route. The nearest is Shoreham which is about 4 miles from Upper Beeding.

Refreshments: The Castle Hotel at Bramber, the Bridge pub and the Rising Sun at Upper Beeding, the Shepherd and Dog at Fulking, the Wheatsheaf pub on the B2116 on the route to Henfield. There are various pubs and cafés in Henfield.

The route: Over half the ride is on relatively level terrain whilst the rest is in undulating country. Six miles of off-road riding along the Downs Link is traffic free but be prepared for muddy patches after wet weather. The route uses the A2037 and the A281 for about 2½ miles.

To extend the ride: Use route 9 from the roundabout at Bramber and continue the ride to Shoreham. **Or:** Use a map to link the ride with route 10.

Turn into Station Road, opposite the Old Railway Tavern, and follow the signs for the Downs Link for the next 5 miles over tracks, bridleway and roads to Bramber. *In detail,* **turn R** at the bottom of Station Road and then **L** immediately into the Downs Link. Ride for 2 miles, crossing the River Adur, drainage ditches and streams as you go. Ride for a further 2 miles or so as the Downs Link curves to

the right, away from the disused railway track and up through farmland. At the top it is worth turning to gaze at the views.

Continue along the track into King's Barn Lane. **Turn L** into King's Stone Avenue. **Turn L** at the T-junction and then continue ahead, away from the major road, along the lane to the roundabout at Bramber. Take the first exit, **L** into Bramber, and pass the Bramber Castle Hotel.

Ride ½ mile through Upper Beeding to the T-junction by the Rising Sun pub. **Turn L** into the A2037 for 1½ miles. There is a gradual climb near Windmill Hill and some good views over countryside as you descend.

Turn R to Edburton and Fulking and ride for about 2¾ miles. This undulating lane at the foot of the Downs offers some wonderful panoramas with the Downs rising to your right and an expanse of Wealden pastures to your left. Pass Tottington Manor Hotel and sail downwards into Edburton. The hamlet was given its name as long ago as AD 950 by Edburga, granddaughter of King Alfred. Consider pausing for a rest at the Shepherd and Dog, which is in the lane's deep fold at the edge of Fulking. This is approximately halfway. Ride through the attractive village.

Turn L, signposted to Clappers

Views over Fulking from the Downs near Devil's Dyke

Lane, at the end of the village (ignore the sharp right hand bend to Poynings). Although the terrain continues to undulate, you ride for 1½ miles along a tranquil shaded lane with hedgerows.

At the pillar box **turn L** into level Holmbush Lane and ride for less than 1½ miles, following the lane as it bends right and becomes Bramlands Lane. **Turn R** at the T-junction, ride up the short hill and **turn R** into the A281.

Turn L, shortly, into Blackstone Lane and ride for nearly a mile. This is another lovely lane, which passes through the delightful village of Blackstone with its timbered and weather-boarded houses.

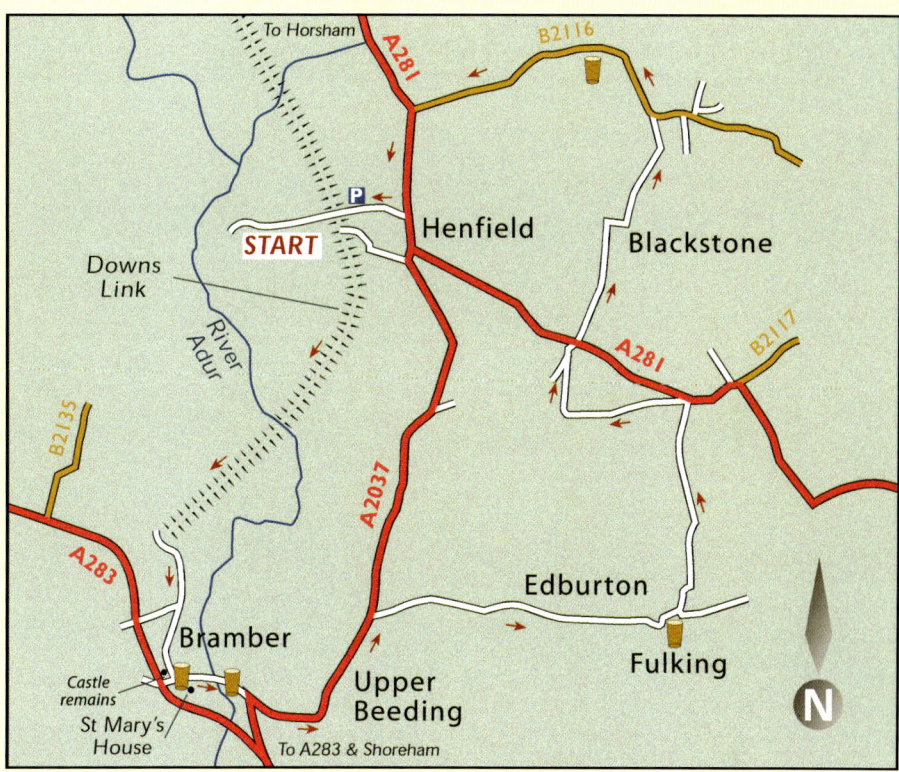

Turn **L** into the B2116, signposted to Henfield, and ride for 2 miles, passing the Wheatsheaf pub on your left. At the T-junction **turn L** into the A281 and ride for 1 mile to Henfield.

Turn **R** into Church Street and soon watch out for the thatched Cat House on your left (see description below). Cycle back to the car park just beyond the Old Railway Tavern on your right.

HENFIELD
Nathaniel Woodward, founder of the schools of Lancing, Ardingly, Hurstpierpoint and St Michael's, Petworth lived here in Victorian times. An eccentric neighbour of Woodward's, a local joiner named Bob Ward, was incensed when Woodward's cat killed his pet canary. He strung wrought iron cats with birds in their mouths around his cottage and rang them loudly when Woodward came by. Much later the cats were recovered and strung around the thatched cottage so that the cottage was named 'Cat House'.

BRAMBER
There is a tall fragment of the old keep at Bramber Castle standing above the village. William the Conqueror originally gave the land to one of his principal lieutenants, William de Braose, who built the castle and a port for shipping as the River Adur then ran at the foot of the

The Cat House at Henfield

castle. Bramber flourished until the 14th century and was an important centre but gradually declined over the years as the river silted up. The centre of the village is now a conservation area. The 15th century St Mary's House is said to be one of the finest timbered houses in Sussex. Formerly run by Benedictine monks who offered a haven for pilgrims en route to Canterbury, it is now open to the public. Only the east wing remains of the original four-sided building with its galleried courtyard. You can see the rare 'shutting window', with its twelve folding sections. The house served as the inspiration for Conan Doyle to write the Sherlock Holmes story The Musgrove Ritual.

FULKING

This is an attractive village with many flint houses, standing at the foot of the Downs. There is a spring-line that follows the line of this road, where chalk meets the clay of the Weald and water cascades by the road where the Pump House stands. This tiny building was part of a 19th century plan to power a hydraulic ram to pump the waters around the village. Just below the spring is the 13th century Shepherd and Dog pub, named after the sheep rearing which has taken place in the area for centuries. Other local villages sent their sheep to be washed; the spring was dammed and the washing was carried out by men standing in the cold water for hours. Expert gangs sheared the sheep and afterwards retired to the Shepherd and Dog, where the earnings were shared.

9

Steyning and Shoreham

14½ or 11¼ miles

Ride from the small country town of Steyning, where the River Adur cuts a gap through the Downs along the river valley to Shoreham and the sea. Follow the scenic lane which undulates along the foot of the Downs past St Botolph's church and on past Lancing College chapel, set on the hill. If you continue to Shoreham Beach, cross the drawbridge to reach the vegetated shingle beach with views of Brighton and Roedean, high on the chalk cliffs. Walk along the River Adur estuary within arm's reach of Shoreham Airport and Helidrome and enjoy the thrill of seeing light aircraft as they come in to land. The return ride crosses the old tollbridge and follows the off-road Coastal Link beside the river and then the Downs Link to Bramber.

Map: OS Landranger 198 Brighton and Lewes (GR 178113).

Starting point: The village hall car park at Steyning. From the A24 Horsham–Worthing road, turn off eastwards at the Washington roundabout onto the A283. In just over 3 miles turn right to Steyning. Turn left opposite the White Horse into Church Lane and follow the lane as it bears right. The car park is shortly on your right after the library.

By train: Shoreham station is on the longer route.

Refreshments: On a sunny day you may wish to buy a picnic, perhaps at a baker's in Shoreham, and eat it on the beach. Alternatively you could try the Sussex Pad Hotel at Lancing for drinks in the conservatory or the Red Lion near Old Shoreham Bridge. At Shoreham Beach there is the Seafood Experience where you can sample seafood – from small tapas-style dishes to seafood platters. The Waterfront pub is also at Shoreham Beach. In Steyning try the café in Cobblers Walk, beneath the clock tower, for cream teas.

The route: Mainly on quiet lanes and on the off-road, but firm surfaced, Downs Link. There is traffic for a short distance through the town in Shoreham but nothing too difficult to negotiate. The road down to Shoreham undulates over the foot of the Downs whilst on the return the Downs Link rises almost imperceptibly. To visit Shoreham Beach, be prepared to push your bike both over the drawbridge and along a footpath for about ½ mile.
To shorten the ride: From Old Shoreham Bridge turn left straight onto the Coastal Link, leaving out Shoreham Beach.
To extend the route: This can be added to route 8 by joining it at Bramber.

43

Turn R out of the car park and follow the road as it climbs and bends left to cross above the Steyning bypass. After the road narrows **turn R** into King's Stone Avenue, signposted 'Downs Link'. **Turn L** at the T-junction and continue straight ahead along a lane as the major road bends right. Ride to the roundabout.

Take the third exit, into Maudlin Lane. Climb a short sharp hill and a view of the Downs opens out to your left. **Turn L** at the T-junction. Follow the lane for about 3½ miles to the A27. You will pass Annington and ride up and down to the little hamlet of Botolphs, which was on one of the early trade routes when tin was taken from Cornwall to Pevensey. Consider a visit to the peaceful church, where there are traces of old wall paintings. Later look to your right where, high on the hill, stands Lancing College chapel, which has the fourth highest interior in the country.

Turn R along Coombes Road just before reaching the traffic lights. The Sussex Pad Hotel is soon on your right and you may consider stopping for a drink in the relaxing conservatory. **Turn L** along the path to the pedestrian lights and cross the A27. Ride straight into the road opposite and pass Shoreham Airport. Cycle over the old tollbridge.

Steyning dates back to the 8th century, according to legend

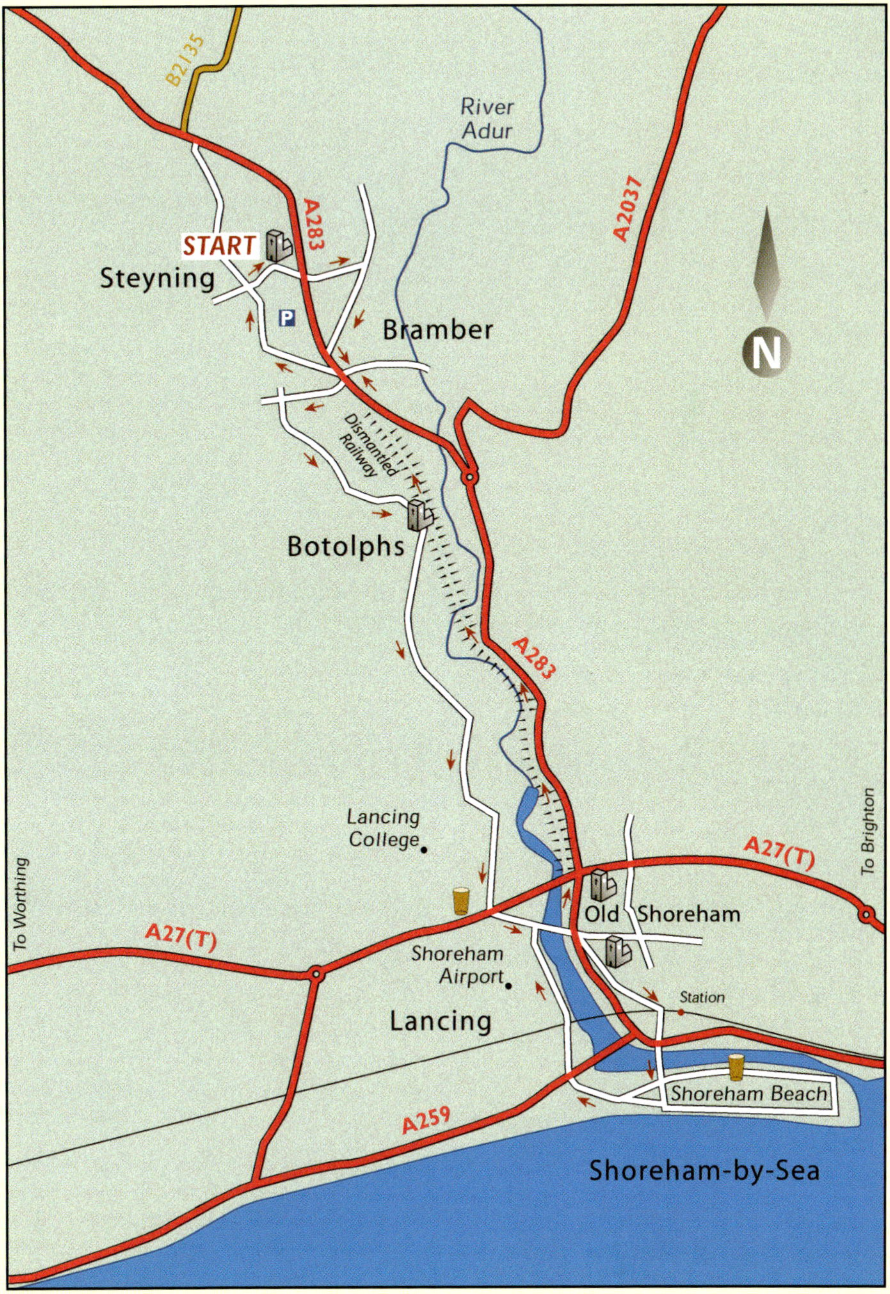

B2135

River
Adur

A283

A2037

START

Steyning

P

Bramber

Dismantled
Railway

Botolphs

A283

Lancing
College

A27(T)

To Brighton

To Worthing

A27(T)

Old Shoreham

Shoreham
Airport

Station

Lancing

A259

Shoreham Beach

Shoreham-by-Sea

N

Shoreham lies at the mouth of the River Adur

If you are taking the shortened route **turn L** into the Coastal Link.

Otherwise cross the A283 to the Red Lion pub. Go through the posts and pass St Nicholas' church on your left. Soon **turn R** into The Street, a cul-de-sac for cars. Cross over the road and cycle into Connaught Avenue and on for nearly ¾ mile, crossing intersections, to a T-junction by Shoreham station.

Turn R across the level crossing and follow the road as it winds into a one-way system past the late Norman parish church. If you wish to visit Marlipins Museum in the High Street, turn right onto the A259, the sea front, and it is in about 200 yards.

Cross straight over the A259 Brighton Road and push your bike over the River Adur by crossing the drawbridge. The harbour is nearby and colourful boats are moored. **Turn L** and the road bends to the right past the Waterfront pub. Cross Riverside Road and the Seafood Experience is shortly on your left. Cross the next intersection and the beach is straight ahead. On a sunny day you can enjoy both a relaxing rest on the beach and the far reaching views towards Brighton and in the other direction to Worthing.

With the beach behind you, **turn L**. When you reach the T-junction **turn L** and shortly **turn R** into Ormonde Way. Soon push your bike up a grassy slope by steps on

your right and cross the road. Push your bike straight into a footpath. Continue straight ahead over the recreation ground, then go under the railway arch to a flagstoned path beside Shoreham Airport.

Go down the steps on your left or walk a little further and cycle down a grassy slope to the airport road. You could visit the Visitor Centre at the Airport and look at memorabilia. Otherwise **turn R** (the runway is to your left). **Turn R** at the road and cycle over Old Shoreham Bridge for the second time.

Turn L into the Coastal Link and ride beside the River Adur for about 2½ miles. After crossing the bridge follow the signs for the Downs Link. In a further ¾ mile **bear L** along the narrow path (still the Downs Link) away from the track as it bends sharply right. Cross the A283 and continue along the Link to Bramber.

At the Bramber roundabout consider a detour into the village of Bramber. See route 8 for places of interest.

From the Link cross The Street and go into Castle Lane ahead, retracing your outward route. **Turn R** into King's Stone Avenue and **turn L** over the bypass to return to the car park. Perhaps finish off the ride with a cream tea at attractive Cobblers Walk in the shadow of the clock tower in the centre of Steyning.

STEYNING

There are many timbered-framed buildings of medieval origin, inviting small shops and the church of St Andrew, by the car park, which is said to have one of the most impressive Norman naves in the country. According to legend the village dates back to the 8th century when St Cuthman pushed his disabled mother in a wheelbarrow from Devon. The barrow broke down at Steyning and this is where St Cuthman remained. The story was used by Christopher Fry, the playwright, as the basis for his play *The Boy with the Cart*. There is a small museum where copies of the conservation area guide may be bought.

SHOREHAM

Shoreham lies at the mouth of the River Adur, which used to be much deeper and wider and navigable all the way to Bramber Castle. The port of Old Shoreham with its wooden tollbridge and church was abandoned as early as 1100 by the Normans as the river silted up. It was the Normans who planned and built New Shoreham as a new town. The fine Norman church of St Mary de Haura (of the harbour) and the Norman customs house, now the Marlipins Museum, in the High Street remain. The shingle on the beach is kept stable by the sea defences offering a rare habitat where particular plants are able to grow. Flowers bloom in profusion in spring and early summer, having evolved to adapt to the harsh exposed environment.

DOWNS LINK

See route 7.

Hurstpierpoint, Clayton and Ditchling

18½ or 23 miles

Travel from Hurstpierpoint, an attractive downland village, along a spectacular lane at the foot of the Downs to the charming village of Clayton. Here there is a beautiful 11th century church with medieval wall paintings. You can make a detour to climb to Jack and Jill, the pair of windmills above the village, and a second detour can be made to Ditchling Beacon at 813 feet with its stunning views. Browse in the sculpture studios on the way to Streat and follow a farm road to picturesque Ditchling. The return ride passes through Hassocks and Keymer, along some idyllic lanes and by the flint buildings of 19th century Hurstpierpoint College, founded by Canon Woodard.

Map: OS Landranger 198 Brighton and Lewes (GR 281165).

Starting point: The car park at Hurstpierpoint. Follow the A23 southwards from Crawley. A mile south of Hickstead turn left on to the B2118 to cross above the A23. At Albourne turn left on to the B2116. Approaching from Brighton, take the A23 northwards. In 1½ miles beyond the Pyecombe service station fork left towards Hurstpierpoint. Turn right over the A23 on to the B2117. Both routes reach the mini-roundabout in the village by the church. Take the Cuckfield road and in a few yards turn right. The car park is shortly on your right opposite the library. If full, alternative parking is available at the Jack and Jill windmills.

By train: Hassocks station is on the route.

Refreshments: Washbrooks Farm in Hurstpierpoint makes an excellent resting place. From the mini-roundabout by the church it is about a third of a mile detour down the B2117, Brighton road. Both the Bull Inn and Dolly's Pantry are at Ditchling.

The route: There are some undulations but it is an easy ride unless you detour to Jack and Jill, or to Ditchling Beacon, which present stiff climbs. There is a stretch of about 3½ miles on the B2116 but traffic is not fast. On the off-road section at Streat you should be prepared to push your bike for ⅓ mile as it is a private road with a footpath.

To visit Jack and Jill windmills: At Clayton ride straight ahead for ½ mile and **turn L** to climb another ½ mile to the windmills. Return the same way and **turn R** into Underhill Lane to join the main route (2 miles).

To visit Ditchling Beacon: At the next crossroads in Underhill Lane **turn R** and climb for about a mile to the Beacon. Return the same way to the crossroads. **Turn R** into Underhill Lane to join the main route (2½ miles).

To extend the route: Use a map to link this ride with route 8.

Jack and Jill windmills, Clayton

Turn L out of the car park and **turn L** again at the mini-roundabout. Ride for about ¾ mile and at the edge of the village **turn R** into New Way Lane. **Turn R** immediately into the single track lane and soon pass Danny, a late 16th century Elizabethan house, visited by Lloyd George and by Churchill, during the two world wars.

This lane is a gem as it winds for 1½ miles along the foot of the Downs with views of Jack and Jill windmills on the skyline. At the T-junction in Clayton you will see Tunnel House, a folly with London to Brighton trains running beneath it. **Turn R** and ride over the bridge.

(A detour is possible to Jack and Jill windmills. See box.)

Turn L into Underhill Lane, signposted to Clayton. After about 1¾ miles you reach a crossroads. (A detour is possible to Ditchling Beacon. See box.) Go straight across and continue riding along Underhill Lane for just over ¾ mile to a T-junction at Westmeston.

Turn R into the B2116. Enjoy a good downhill run past Middleton Manor and in less than a mile **turn L**, signposted to Streat. Watch for the interesting Skelton Sculpture Studios on your left where you can browse, if open. Cycle up the hill

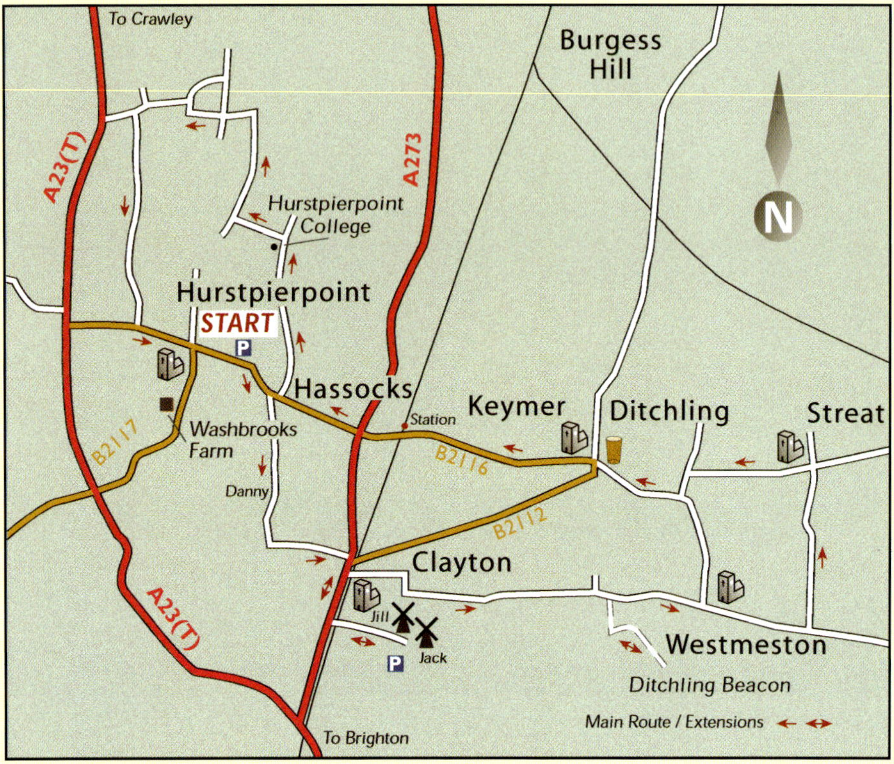

To Crawley

Burgess Hill

A23(T)

A273

Hurstpierpoint College

N

Hurstpierpoint

START
P

Hassocks

Keymer

Ditchling

Streat

Station

Washbrooks Farm

B2117

B2116

Danny

B2112

Clayton

Jill

A23(T)

Jack
P

Westmeston

Ditchling Beacon

Main Route / Extensions

To Brighton

and **turn sharp L** immediately before Streat church along the private road. Push your bike for about ⅓ mile as it is a footpath.

Go down the hill and **turn L** and immediately **R** along the bridleway on the farm road. **Turn L** at the T-junction and soon **R** onto the B2116, signposted to Ditchling.

Continue on the B2116, for about 2 miles, through Keymer and Hassocks. Cross the A273 at the traffic lights and in a further ¾ mile **turn R** into College Road. Cycle for nearly a mile as far as the flint buildings of Hurstpierpoint College.

Turn L by the school. As the lane bends to the left, **turn R** into Danworth Lane. Looking back, the spire of Hurstpierpoint church can be seen high on the horizon. In ¾ mile, at the top of a hill, **turn L**.

Cross over into Pomper Lane, a wonderful downhill run along a quiet winding lane for ¼ mile. **Turn L** and in ½ mile **turn L** again opposite a thatched cottage, and next to a stream, into Langton Lane. There is a gradual climb towards Hurstpierpoint.

Turn L at the T-junction and cycle to the roundabout in the village. **Turn L** and then **R** for the car park.

Views to Dtichling and beyond from Ditchling Beacon

HURSTPIERPOINT

Hurst means 'wooded hill' and is often used in Sussex place names. De Pierpoint was the name of a Norman family who settled here during the reign of William the Conqueror and descendants of the family remained until the 15th century. Hurstpierpoint is now a lively village with some elegant Georgian architecture, a good variety of small shops and a café. There is a 19th century church where medieval effigies of a defaced templar and a nameless knight can be found in the south transept and the north aisle.

CLAYTON

For such a small village picturesque Clayton has many claims to fame. The 1¼ mile Clayton rail tunnel was a remarkable engineering feat in the mid 19th century. The area is perhaps best known for the two 19th century windmills called Jack and Jill, high on the downs. Jack is a black tower mill whilst Jill is a smaller, wooden post mill. Both were moved from Dyke Road, Brighton to the present site by a team of oxen. Jill is sometimes open to the public. The Norman church of St John is beautiful and renowned for its remarkable wall paintings, which may date back to the 12th century.

DITCHLING

This attractive village at the foot of the Downs has a church dating from the 13th century and some timber-framed houses, for example, the so-called Anne of Cleves House opposite the church. Ditchling Museum has exhibitions and shows village life through the centuries back to Saxon times.

51

Weir Wood Reservoir, West Hoathly and Horsted Keynes

21 or 14 miles

The High Weald offers a ride to satisfy a wide range of interests. Weir Wood Reservoir and its island are home to many species of birds and you may see a heron, a visiting cormorant or perhaps a resting migrant osprey in autumn. Just ½ mile from the route is Standen, a National Trust owned family house and a showpiece of William Morris designs (entrance fee). Travel along the disused railway line, Worth Way, climb to Turners Hill and continue to the attractive village of West Hoathly with its old Priest House. Sweep down the long descent to the Bluebell Railway at Horsted Keynes where vintage steam trains run between Kingscote and Sheffield Park. The return ride climbs into Ashdown Forest, where you can see glorious views before the exhilarating downhill run back to the reservoir.

Map: OS Landranger 187 Dorking and Reigate (GR 383342).

Starting point: The car park at Weir Wood Reservoir. From East Grinstead take the B2110 in the direction of Turners Hill. In less than a mile from the outskirts of the town turn left at the crossroads into Saint Hill Road. Turn right at the junction into West Hoathly Road and in about 1¼ miles, at the base of a steep hill by the reservoir, turn left into Legsheath Lane. The car park is nearly ½ mile on the left.

By train: Horsted Keynes station on the Bluebell Railway is on the route.

Refreshments: If you visit Standen there is a National Trust restaurant. The Royal Oak is at Crawley Down and Tulleys Farm Tea Room is near Turners Hill. The Cat, at West Hoathly, nearly halfway, is a good place to rest. Both the Green Man and the Crown are at Horsted Keynes by the green.

The route: This is a hilly route but there are wonderful long downhills. There is an easy 3 mile, off-road section on the Worth Way and some fast traffic around the Turners Hill area for about 3 miles.
To shorten the route: Use the main route as far as Horsted Keynes station. Then take the Bluebell Railway to Kingscote station. **Turn R** out of the station to reach the B2110 then **turn R** and continue for 1 mile. **Turn R** to Weir Wood Reservoir and the car park (14 miles). Timetable information: 01825 722370 (24 hours) or 01825 720801 (office hours).
To extend the route: Use a map to link the ride with route 13.

Turn R out of the car park and **R** again at the T-junction. Climb the hill and cycle past Deer's Leap cycle trails.

Consider taking a detour to Standen (½ mile to the house itself) by continuing ahead up a hill and following the signs to Standen on your right. This National Trust property has a restaurant where you can sit and enjoy a drink after viewing the house and grounds. Return to the same point to rejoin the route.

Turn L into Saint Hill Road and climb the hill past Saint Hill Manor. Ride down to the crossroads, go straight over into Imberhorne Lane and ride for 1 mile.

Turn L into a pathway just before a bridge, signposted 'NCN 21', and follow the Worth Way for about 3½ miles. This is the disused branch line that used to run between East Grinstead and Three Bridges. Although the Way is interrupted at Crawley Down continue to follow the signs for NCN 21 through the housing estate and over the crossroads, keeping the shops to your right. Ride into the Worth Way as it continues at the end of Old Station Road.

Turn L at a road crossing. In just over ¼ mile **turn L** at the T-junction, signposted to Turners Hill, and cycle up Major's Hill. Tulleys Farm Shop and Tea Room is on your right in about a mile. **Turn L** at the T-junction soon after the

In the gardens of the Old Priest House, West Hoathly

To East Grinstead
& to A23

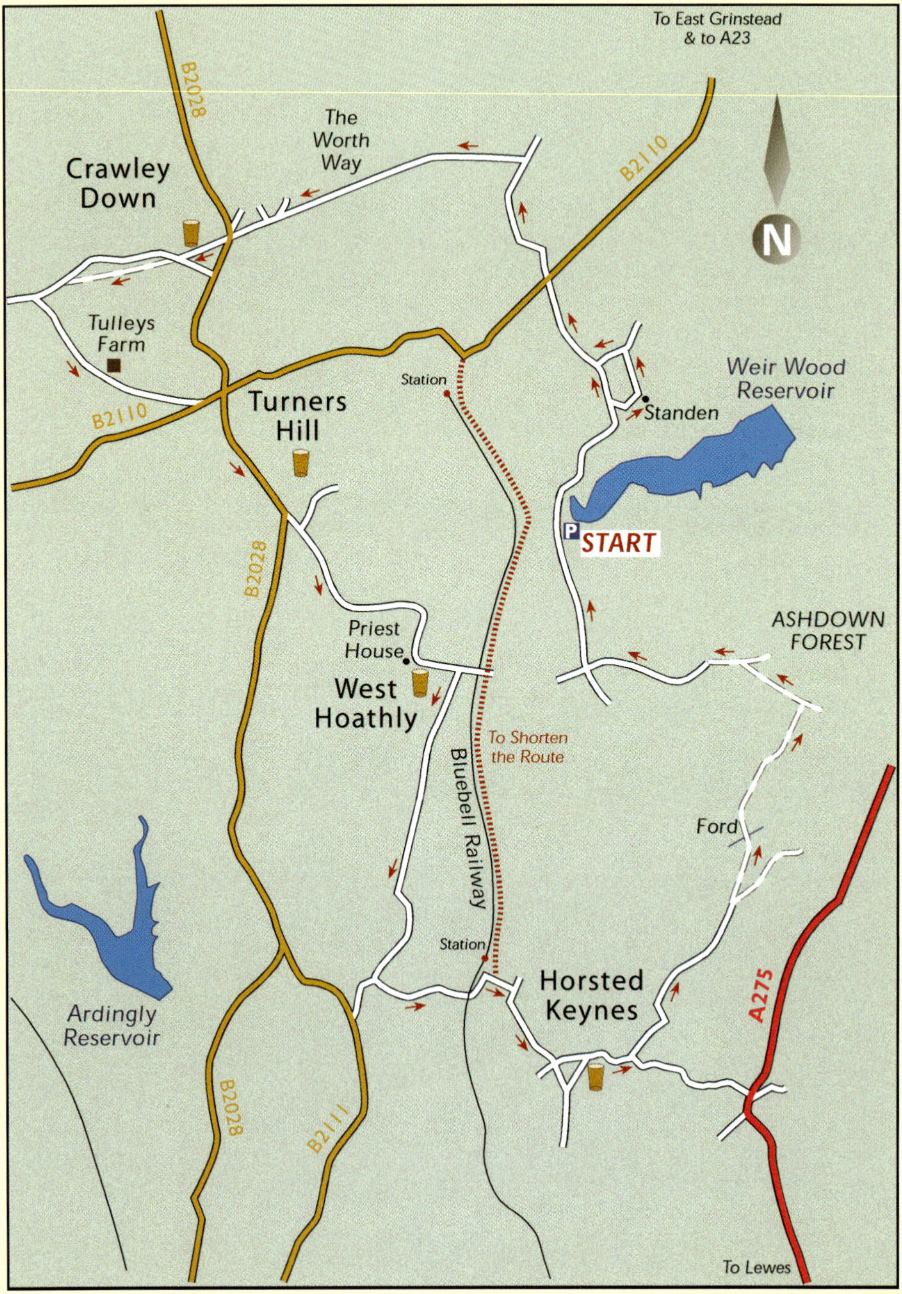

B2028

The
Worth
Way

**Crawley
Down**

B2110

N

Tulleys
Farm

B2110

**Turners
Hill**

Station

Weir Wood
Reservoir

Standen

B2028

P **START**

ASHDOWN
FOREST

Priest
House

**West
Hoathly**

*To Shorten
the Route*

Bluebell Railway

Ford

Ardingly
Reservoir

Station

**Horsted
Keynes**

A275

B2028

B2111

To Lewes

19th century church of St Leonard to the crossroads at Turners Hill. There are two pubs and an antique shop as well as good views to the north.

Turn R into the B2028 for a mile. **Bear L** and cycle for nearly 1½ miles. **Turn R** to the village of West Hoathly. As this is about halfway, perhaps pause for refreshment at the Cat pub where there are often welcoming candles on the tables. **Turn L** by the pub unless you are visiting the picturesque Priest House which is a little further on the right (entrance fee).

Turn R just before Vignols Cross Inn and enjoy a long downhill ride for 2 miles and some wonderful panoramic views to Ashdown Forest, interrupted by only a short climb. **Turn L** and follow the signs to Horsted Keynes. The station on the famed Bluebell Line with its vintage steam trains is about 1¼ miles on your left. Ride for a further 1¼ miles and **bear L** at the junction to reach the village. Both the Green Man and the Crown offer views onto the green and a further opportunity for a rest.

Fork L at the end of the village and cycle up Birchgrove Road with its gentle gradient for 2 miles. **Turn L**, signposted to Twyford, and follow the tranquil lane to offset crossroads. Ride across and sweep downwards to the ford. Climb steeply upwards for 1¼ miles

through Ashdown Forest, noticing a house with three unusual chimney stacks as you pass.

Turn L and ride for ¾ mile, perhaps stopping to admire the views from this Ashdown Forest ridge. Cross straight over at the crossroads into Legsheath Lane and sail down the hill for 1½ miles to the Weir Wood Reservoir car park, which is on your right.

WEIR WOOD RESERVOIR
This 280 acre area of water, formed by the damming of one of the headstreams of the River Medway in 1950, lies just inside the East Sussex boundary and has been designated as a Site of Special Scientific Interest. The reservoir, with its central island, forms a beautiful expanse of water that serves as a magnet to many species of bird. Cormorants visit from the coast, in spring you may witness the courtship dance of the great crested grebe and in winter wildfowl such as wigeon and goldeneye from Siberia may be seen.

WEST HOATHLY
The village sits high in the Weald at 600 feet and is on the edge of the Ashdown Forest. There are several attractive timber-framed houses, and the Priest House, which dates from the 15th century, is well known. It is now a museum created by the Sussex Archaeological Society with an English country garden. The church of St Margaret of Antioch is opposite and has an unusual churchyard with six terraces.

BLUEBELL RAILWAY
See route 12.

Ditchling Common, Sheffield Park and the Bluebell Railway

24 miles

The route undulates through the pastures and woods of the High Weald and crosses and recrosses the boundary between East and West Sussex. A highlight of the ride is the National Trust owned Sheffield Park Garden (entrance fee) with its chain of lakes, cascades and spectacular variety of trees famous for their autumn colours. Nearby at Sheffield Park station the engines of the Bluebell Railway offer a reminder of the great days of steam. Pass through the attractive village of Fletching, and at Newick consider a pause for refreshment at the reputedly haunted Bull Inn, where you can watch for the strange ball-like object which is said to roll across the floor of the bar from nowhere to nowhere.

Map: OS Landranger 198 Brighton and Lewes (GR 338182).

Starting point: The car park at Ditchling Common Country Park. Ditchling Common is well signposted from Burgess Hill. Follow the B2113 past the railway station and continue for 1½ miles. Cross the B2112 and the Country Park is shortly on your left, indicated with a brown sign.

By train: Sheffield Park on the Bluebell Line is on the route. Burgess Hill station is less than 2 miles from Ditchling Common Country Park.

Refreshments: If you are looking for refreshment in the first part of the ride you could make a short detour to Haywards Heath. In the second half there are many options. Oak Hall Manor, next door to Sheffield Park, has a buffet restaurant and tea garden which serves a wide choice of meals and snacks. At Sheffield Park station there is Puffers, a self-service restaurant, also the Bessemer Arms, a replica Victorian pub. The Rose and Crown and the Griffin Inn are at Fletching and the Bull, the 16th century Royal Oak and the Green Man are at Newick. A short footpath from Green Lane, near South Common, Chailey, will take you to Horns Lodge, an inn offering pizza, or to the well-stocked village shop and post office close by. The Plough is at Hattons Green.

The route: A ride with plenty of ups and downs but the hills are not usually very long and many of the lanes are extremely quiet. There is a 2 mile return trip on the A275 to visit Sheffield Park and the Bluebell Railway and about ¾ mile on the same road at South Common, Chailey. There is a short off-road section along a bridleway at South Street which is generally well surfaced but has the odd muddy patch.

Turn L from the car park and in less than a mile, after a short downhill run **turn L** signposted Wivelsfield, into quiet Hundred Acre Lane. In less than 1½ miles **bear L**, signposted to Haywards Heath, and shortly **L** again at the T-junction.

In just over ¼ mile **turn R** into delightful Slugwash Lane and ride the undulations for about 3 miles. The Sussex Border Path follows the course of the lane for nearly a mile so you are straddling the borders of East and West Sussex. Watch for the 'Cottage of Content' on the right, complete with hollyhocks in summer. After a climb **turn R** into the A272. In a few yards **turn L** into the B2111, signposted to Lindfield. There is a good downhill sweep towards Walstead for ½ mile. **Turn R**, signposted to Freshfield. Soon **turn R** opposite the cemetery and shortly enjoy views to Ashdown Forest on the left. Continue for nearly 2½ miles as you pass the unusual model at East Mascalls Farm and ride under the railway bridge at Freshfields.

At a junction, first **bear L** at the signpost and at the T-junction cross the major road into Ketche's Lane. Cycle for 2 miles and cross the A275. On the corner is 'Trading Boundaries' which you may consider visiting. It claims to have the largest collection of ethnic furniture, antiques and handicrafts in the UK. Your route will be ahead after visiting Sheffield Park.

Sheffield Park is colourful at any time of year

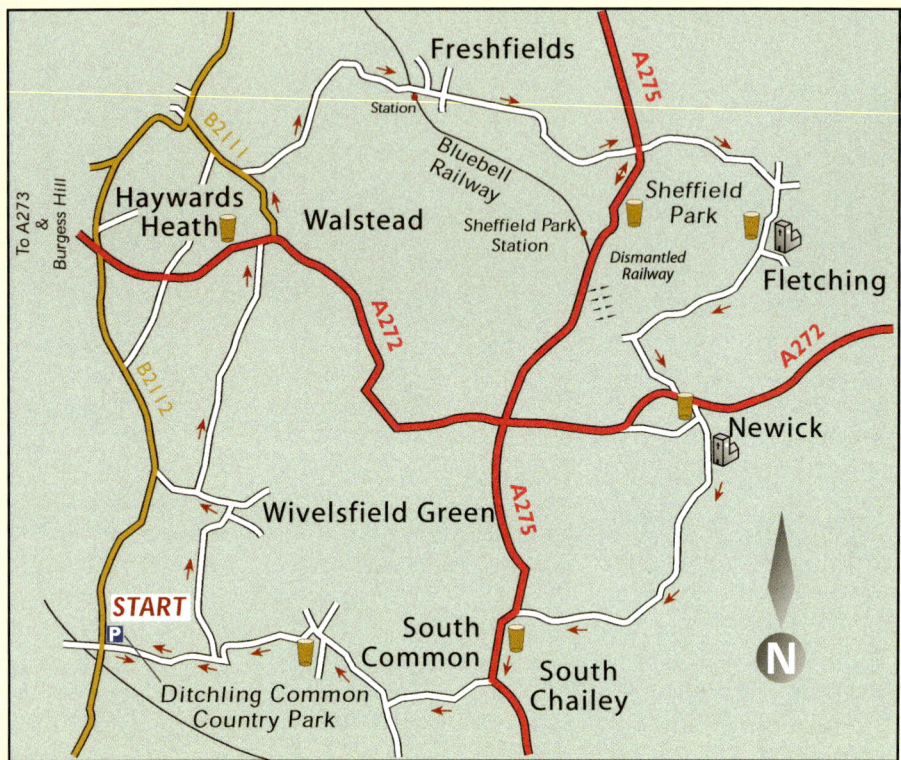

To visit Sheffield Park and the Bluebell Railway: Turn R into the A275 and the entrance to Sheffield Park is ½ mile on your left. Ride up the driveway and perhaps pause for refreshment at Oak Hall Manor with its hanging greenery, stained glass and panelled walls. The park entrance is a little further along the drive. For Sheffield Park station continue for a further ½ mile on the A275 and the Bluebell Railway is on your right. Return to the crossroads and join the route by **turning R** in the direction of Fletching.

In 2 miles you reach the half way point and the attractive village of Fletching with its two pubs. In medieval times it was known for the manufacture of the arrowheads that helped to win the Battles of Crecy and Agincourt for England. In addition Simon de Montfort spent a night of vigil in the 13th century village church before his defeat of Henry III at the Battle of Lewes.

Turn R opposite the church into Mill Lane. **Turn L** in 1½ miles at the junction in the direction of Newick. **Turn L** at the T-junction into the A272. Soon **turn R** at the triangular Newick village green,

Sheffield Park Station on the Bluebell Line

where there is a long-handled pump, installed at Queen Victoria's Diamond Jubilee in 1897. You will see the plaque which warns against filling steam engines! There are no less than three pubs to choose from in the next ¼ mile. Ride on past the church at the top of a rise for about ¾ mile.

Turn R at the T-junction in the direction of Lewes and shortly **turn L** in the direction of Chailey. Continue for 2½ miles along Marstakes Lane, enjoying the good downhill sweep at the start.

Turn L into Green Lane immediately before the T-junction with the A275. **Turn L** at Setford's Field into the bridleway past Cameridge Farmhouse. In about ¼ mile watch for the brickworks and **turn R** into the bridleway through the works down to the A275. (To visit the Horns Lodge or the village shop on the main road, **turn R** opposite Setford's Field into a footpath. Return to the same point if you wish to minimise your ride on the A275.)

After the brickworks, **turn L** into the A275 for a few yards and then **turn R** into Mill Lane, signposted to Wivelsfield Green, and cycle for a mile as it changes to Honeypot Lane. **Turn R**, signposted to Wivelsfield, for over ¾ mile. **Turn L**, signposted to Burgess Hill, just *after* passing the Plough, and follow the road for 2 miles back to the car park.

● ●

BLUEBELL RAILWAY

The line runs currently from Kingscote in the north to Sheffield Park station in the south. The trains are pulled by steam engines along the restored section of the old East Grinstead to Lewes line through beautiful Sussex countryside where bluebells abound in spring. Walk back in time into the engine shed at Sheffield Park to find the sights and sounds of railways as they once were. Smell the coal, hear the hiss of steam, see an inspection pit and a water crane and admire the engines awaiting their restoration. A small exhibits museum and model railway are added attractions. Telephone: 01825 720800.

SHEFFIELD PARK GARDEN

Sheffield Park was originally mentioned as far back as the Domesday Book and has a history which includes a visit by Henry VIII in 1538. This landscaped garden was laid out in the 18th century by Capability Brown and Humphry Repton for the first Earl of Sheffield and was developed further in the early years of the 20th century. It is now National Trust owned, although the house, which is seen from the grounds, is in private ownership. There are acres of rare trees and shrubs, which offer outstanding autumn colour. Four lakes are linked by cascades and waterfalls. Spring and early summer are beautiful times with daffodils and carpets of bluebells followed by azaleas and rhododendrons. Bicycles may be left whilst you explore the garden. Telephone: 01825 791264 for opening hours.

13

Forest Row, Groombridge and Ashdown Forest

15½ or 22 miles

The route follows Forest Way, a disused railway line with an excellent surface, which runs through pastoral countryside to Groombridge in Kent. In Groombridge perhaps visit the Spa Valley Railway or enjoy Groombridge Place Gardens where there is a 17th century moated manor house with walled gardens and an 'enchanted forest' (entrance fee). Alternatively just rest at the Crown Inn and soak up the atmosphere of Old Groombridge with picturesque 18th century tiled cottages round the village green. For an easy ride, return along Forest Way or, for those who wish to stretch their legs, climb into the Ashdown Forest for a bird's eye view of the surrounding countryside.

Map: OS Landranger 187 Dorking and Reigate and 188 Maidstone and the Weald of Kent (GR 427351). There is a Forest Way leaflet available from Visitor Information: 01825 713862.

Starting point: The car park at Forest Row. Take the A22 East Grinstead–Eastbourne road. At the mini-roundabout on the north side of Forest Row, just under 3 miles from East Grinstead, turn off on the B2110. Turn first left into Station Road, immediately after the Foresters Arms, and the car park is on your left.

By train: East Grinstead is 3 miles from the route. Groombridge station on the Spa Valley Railway line is close to the route (limited service) and Eridge station is within 1 mile.

Refreshments: There are some excellent pubs in this area. The Anchor Inn at Hartfield and the Dorset Arms near Withyham are quite close to Forest Way. The Crown Inn at Old Groombridge, by the green, has home-made food and nearby Burrswood serves light meals and teas. In the Ashdown Forest there is the Hatch Inn and teas and coffees are available at Wych Cross Nurseries.

The route: Forest Way is off-road and relatively level from Forest Row to Groombridge and follows part of NCN 21. For a gentle, relaxed ride take the option to retrace your outward route along the Way.

To extend the route: A more energetic alternative for the return ride is to climb from Hartfield to the Ashdown Forest along the B2026. This involves about 5 miles of undulating countryside and climbs to the Hatch Inn, near Coleman's Hatch, and Wych Cross. Beyond the Hatch Inn there is some faster traffic for 4 miles. There is a fine descent down Priory Road to Forest Row for over 2 miles.

From the car park exit, **turn L** to cross the lane and go into the play area. Take a diagonal course downwards across the grass. Go between the wooden posts in the corner of the park to a T-junction of paths. **Turn L** and follow the bridleway across the bridge and up to Forest Way.

Turn R by the colourful board depicting Forest Way and continue for about 6¾ miles to the B2110, not far from Groombridge. The ride runs along the Medway valley floodplain where there are good views of the hills above.

On the way you ride under an archway and reach a crossing lane where there is the option of making a short detour to Hartfield by **turning R** and then **L** into the B2026. At a second intersection near Balls Green you may detour by **turning R** and **R** again, to visit Withyham with its quaint tile-hung houses and the atmospheric Dorset Arms.

Forest Way meets the B2110 after a downward slope. Cross over and continue on the track, NCN 21, for 1 mile. You will cross the B2188 and go under a railway bridge. **Turn L** at a T-junction, climb Corseley Road and follow the sharp right hand bend to coast down the other side to Groombridge.

To make a short detour to the Spa Valley Railway: Turn R by the post office on the corner in Groombridge and ride up Station Road past the bakery. The old station, now used as offices, is on

Autumn colours in Ashdown Forest

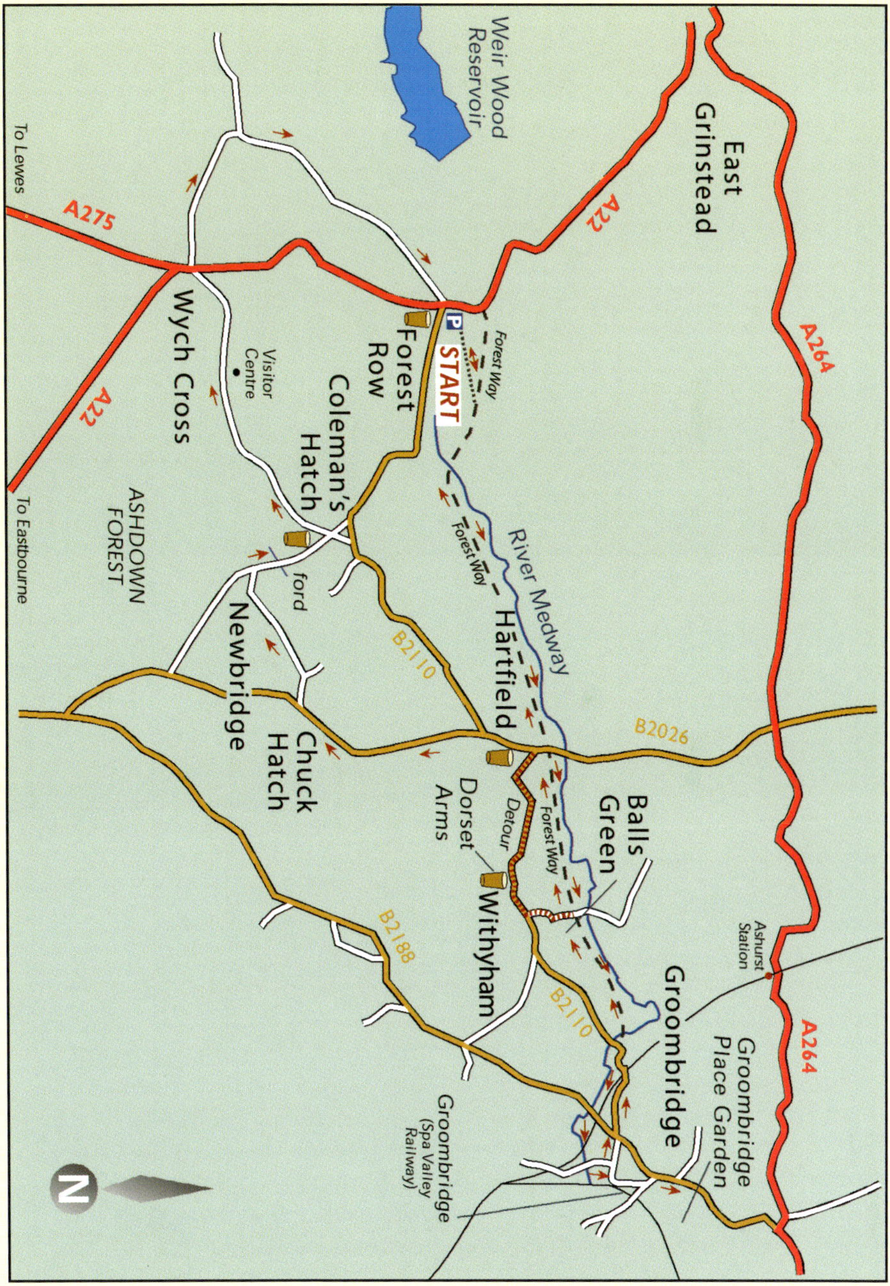

Weir Wood Reservoir

East Grinstead

A275

To Lewes

A22

A22

To Eastbourne

Wych Cross

Visitor Centre

ASHDOWN FOREST

Forest Row

Coleman's Hatch

ford

Newbridge

Chuck Hatch

B2110

P START

Forest Way

Forest Way

Forest Way

River Medway

Hartfield

Dorset Arms

Detour

Withyham

B2188

B2110

Balls Green

B2026

Forest Way

Ashurst Station

Groombridge

Groombridge Place Garden

A264

A264

Groombridge (Spa Valley Railway)

N

One of Forest Way's colourful signs

your left before the bridge. Go through the gate on the left of the building and along the platform to see the steam train which runs to Tunbridge Wells. Telephone: 01892 537715 for operating times.

Otherwise **turn L** by the post office and go to the mini-roundabout. Take the second exit into the B2110 and Groombridge Place Gardens is shortly on your right. Telephone: 01892 861444 for opening times. Old Groombridge is a little further up Groombridge Hill. Here you can enjoy a rest at the Crown Inn, bedecked with flowers in summer.

Return the way you came to the top of the hill on Corseley Road. Go to the mini-roundabout, take the first exit into the village, **turn R** by the post office and climb the hill past the school.

At the top go straight on along the unmade road, Florence Lane, which is also a bridleway. **Turn L** into the B2110 and ride for nearly a mile. **Turn R** into Forest Way, retracing the outward route for about 2½ miles to Hartfield.

Either: Take the gentler route via Forest Way back to Forest Row, perhaps making a detour to Hartfield here, if you didn't do this earlier.

Or: Return via Ashdown Forest. **Turn L** into the lane and **turn L** again to ride along the B2026 to Hartfield. At the junction **turn R**. Soon you are in the centre of the village with the inviting Anchor Inn on your left. Ride through the village and shortly **fork L** still on the B2026. Cycle along the undulating road for about 1½ miles. **Turn R**, after the sign for Chuck Hatch, signposted to Newbridge, and keep ahead (ignoring the right hand turning in ¼ mile). This attractive lane follows the boundary of Ashdown Forest in places. In nearly a mile watch out for the ford at the bottom of the hill by the road junction.

Turn R and climb for ¾ mile to the Hatch Inn. Perhaps rest here for a while in the garden. Leave the Hatch and **turn L**. The road climbs gradually, passing several viewpoints where you can get off and gaze at panoramic views. In about 1½ miles watch for the Ashdown Forest Information Centre on your right. Housed in a Sussex Barn it has a small exhibition and leaflets about various aspects of the forest. Ride on to Wych Cross Nurseries where there is the opportunity for tea.

Cross the A22 at Wych Cross traffic lights. In just over a mile **turn R** into Priory Road, signposted to Forest Row, for more than 2 miles of a superb downhill run into the village. Take the second exit at the mini-roundabout and the car park is just after the Foresters Arms on your left.

FOREST WAY

In 1855 a branch line was opened from Three Bridges to East Grinstead and later extended to Tunbridge Wells. It survived a century, only to be closed by Dr Beeching who was not only a local resident and user of the line but also Chairman of British Railways. The disused part of the line from East Grinstead to Groombridge became a linear country park known as Forest Way, which is home to various species of wildlife including badgers, foxes and swallows. Forest Way is also part of the National Cycle Network running from London to Eastbourne.

HARTFIELD

This is an especially attractive village with half-timbered, tile-hung and weather-boarded houses, just a mile or so from the northern boundary of Ashdown Forest. A.A. Milne, author of the Winnie the Pooh books, lived here and the forest is the setting for many of the stories. Pooh Bridge, where Winnie the Pooh played Pooh-Sticks, is in Posingford Wood and and Five Hundred Acre Wood is also close by. If children are with you consider a visit to Pooh Corner, a shop in the village that sells all manner of 'Pooh-phernalia'

14

Piltdown, Glynde and Isfield

21 or 17 miles

This is a rural route with places of interest scattered along the way. They include Glyndebourne, famous for its opera, the Bradness Art Gallery and the Lavender Line at Isfield. Ride up into downland scenery from Ringmer village green and coast past Glyndebourne Opera House, which is followed by a farm where you may see alpacas grazing. You can choose to detour to the attractive village of Glynde, lying in the shadow of Mount Caburn, where you can glimpse the imposing entrance to Glyndebourne Place and visit the unusual Palladian church. Later you come to the Bentley Wildfowl and Motor Museum, which exhibits veteran and vintage cars and boasts the largest private collection of wildfowl in the country, whilst the village of Isfield is the home of the Lavender Line. Here you can visit a working railway museum or book for a trip on the footplate.

Map: OS Landranger 198 Brighton and Lewes (GR 450215).

Starting point: The car park at the Peacock Inn at Shortbridge, south-east of Piltdown. Take the A272 between Haywards Heath and the A22 at Maresfield. Turn off just east of the Piltdown Man pub and the car park is in about a mile on the left hand side, opposite the Peacock Inn.

By train: Glynde station is near the route at the far end of Glynde village.

Refreshments: The Anchor Inn at Barcombe, gloriously sited on the River Ouse, the Cock, just off the A26 Lewes/Uckfield road, the tea room at Glynde Place when the house is open, the Laughing Fish at Isfield and the Peacock Inn itself. If you visit the Bentley Wildfowl and Motor Museum (entrance fee) there is a tea room which specialises in home-made cakes.

The route: The area round Ringmer is fairly flat but the rest of the ride is undulating. The hills are not usually very long, however, and most give way to good downhill runs. The lanes are mostly quiet. You cross and recross the A26 and follow it for about ¼ mile where you can push your bike on the wide grass verge beside it. There is ½ mile on the B2192, where the traffic is quite fast.
To shorten the route: From the outskirts of Ringmer continue along Norlington Lane (ignoring the main route, which turns to the right) and into Green Lane. Rejoin the route at Harvey's Lane in about 2½ miles. This shortens the main route (not including the detours to the Anchor and to Glynde) by 4 miles.
To extend the route: Detour to the Anchor Inn by turning off the route north of Barcombe Cross. Or: Detour to the village of Glynde. Or: Use a map to link with route 12.

Turn R out of the Peacock car park and ride up the hill and past the golf course (ignore the turning to the golf club itself) to Piltdown Pond. **Turn L**, signposted to Barcombe, and ride for 2¼ miles to a T-junction. This is an attractive, undulating lane and at Sharpsbridge you cross the River Ouse.

Turn L at the T-junction and continue for about 3 miles to the village of Barcombe Cross. On the way, as you sail down an incline at Spithurst, watch for the Bradness Art Gallery on your left where you are welcome to browse through the landscape paintings. The Anchor Inn is in a wonderful peaceful backwater by the River Ouse and can be reached by turning left ½ mile before reaching Barcombe Cross. It is a detour of just over 3 miles return.

Take the first exit at the mini-roundabout at Barcombe Cross village. Ride for 2 miles to the T-junction with the A26, passing Barcombe Mills, where a flour mill once stood by the River Ouse.

Turn R into the A26 for less than ¼ mile. It is suggested that you cross over and push your bike past the organic farm on the wide verge. Just past the farm recross the road and look for a grassy path which slopes gently down to the attractive Cock pub, where you may decide to rest.

Cycle along the lane past the pub and **turn R** at the T-junction to ride parallel with the A26. Shortly, just past Goldcliff Nurseries, **turn L** onto the paved way across the verge to the main road. Cross straight over the A26 and into the road opposite

The opera house at Glyndebourne is passed on the route

67

To A22

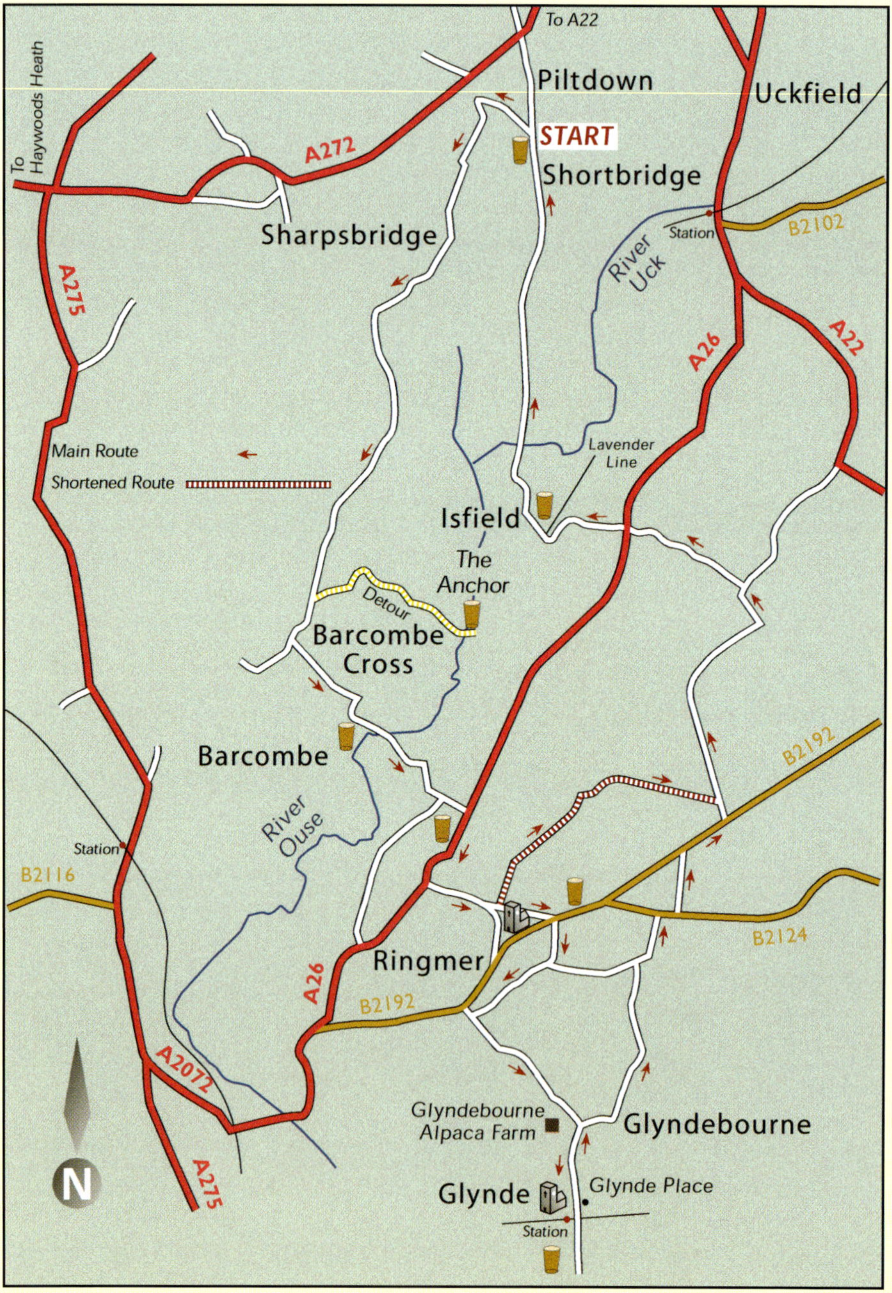

Piltdown

Uckfield

START

Shortbridge

To Haywoods Heath

A272

Sharpsbridge

B2102

Station

River Uck

A275

A26

A22

Main Route

Shortened Route

Lavender Line

Isfield

The Anchor

Detour

Barcombe Cross

Barcombe

B2192

River Ouse

Station

B2116

B2124

A26

Ringmer

B2192

A2072

Glyndebourne Alpaca Farm

Glyndebourne

N

A275

Glynde

Glynde Place

Station

in the direction of Ringmer.

Turn L in ½ mile and immediately L again.

To shorten the route: Continue ahead (see box above).

Otherwise: Turn R into Bishops Lane, signposted to Ringmer. Soon Ringmer village green is to your right, bordered by old cottages and the 14th century church of St Mary. Continue along the lane to the B2192. Cross over and go into Harrisons Lane to ride for a mile past Ringmer School and into Gote Lane, where views of the Downs unfold.

Turn L at the T-junction and climb gradually upwards with stunning vistas to be seen on all sides. Sail downwards but watch for Glyndebourne on your left.

For the detour to Glynde: Ride ahead past the alpaca farm for about a mile. Just over the brow of the hill the impressive entrance to Glynde Place is on your left. After enjoying Glynde, and perhaps visiting the Trevor Arms beyond the station, retrace the route to the alpaca farm. To join the main route **turn R** into Moor Lane.

Otherwise: Turn L along Moor Lane opposite Glyndebourne Alpaca Farm. The route now lies along some tranquil lanes. Cycle along Moor Lane for a mile. **Turn L** opposite the post box and in just

over ½ mile **bear R** at the next post box. **Turn R** into the B2124 and soon **L** into Half Mile Drove.

Turn R into the B2192 and in less than ½ mile **turn L** into Harveys Lane. Follow the lane for just over 3 miles by farmland and woods to crossroads and the A26. On your way you will see Bentley Wildlife and Motor Museum after 1½ miles and in a further mile **bear L** at the junction, signposted to Isfield, and cycle to the crossroads.

Cross the A26 and ride to Isfield. **Turn R** by the station and perhaps visit the Lavender Line Museum. Continue your ride through Isfield village, past the old mill.

In 2½ miles from the station, **turn L**, signposted to Piltdown, and go down the hill **bearing L** at the bottom. The thatched Peacock Inn is on your left.

●●●●●●●●●●●●●●●●●●●●●●●

BARCOMBE
This consists of three communities that have become scattered. The area around the church was deserted after the bubonic plague in the 17th century and Barcombe Cross became the village centre. Barcombe Mills is by the River Ouse.

GLYNDE
The small village of Glynde lies at the foot of Mount Caburn, an Iron Age fort. Perhaps its greatest claim to fame is the Elizabethan Glynde Place, which has remained in the same family for 400 years. Telephone: 01273 858224 for opening times.

Arlington Reservoir, Cuckmere Haven and Wilmington

20 or 12 miles

The ride follows the Cuckmere River through Seven Sisters Country Park to the estuary at Cuckmere Haven. Enjoy the contrast of tiny unspoilt villages and flint churches with popular Drusilla's Park and the lively bustle of picturesque Alfriston. You can ride along the valley through the Country Park to the shingle beach at Cuckmere Haven where the view of imposing chalk white cliffs offers a taste of the unique coastal scenery of the Seven Sisters area.

Map: OS Landranger 199 Eastbourne and Hastings (GR 527074).

Starting point: Arlington Reservoir pay and display car park. Take the A27 between Lewes and Polegate. At a roundabout approximately 8 miles from Lewes turn off for Berwick. Cross the level crossing by Berwick station and Arlington Reservoir is ½ mile further on the right. The small, but free, car park at Wilmington Priory is an alternative.

By train: Berwick station is on the route.

Refreshments: There are many options in Alfriston from pubs to tea rooms whilst at Litlington there are tea gardens at the nursery and the Plough and Harrow pub. Exceat Farmhouse Restaurant has a walled courtyard for outdoor eating. Wilmington has the Wishing Well Tea Room with its home-made cakes as well as the Giant's Rest pub. At Arlington there is the Yew Tree Inn.

The route: There are some undulations but the area offers relatively easy riding. The exception is the mile climb from Litlington on the way to Wilmington but there are some stunning views and a visit to Lullington church provides a break on the climb. You retrace the outward ride on the 4 miles from Litlington to Cuckmere Haven but it is a delightful area. There is a surfaced path in the Seven Sisters Country Park with a short distance of unsurfaced, but firm, track to the beach.

To shorten the ride: Cross the Cuckmere River at Alfriston and **turn R** with the main route. Then **turn L** at the Lullington T-junction to omit Exceat and the Seven Sisters Country Park. This saves about 8 miles.

To extend the route: The ride can be linked to route 16 by using NCN 2 to Polegate from 1½ miles north of the A27 at Wilmington.

Turn L out of Arlington Reservoir and ride for about 1½ miles, going over the level crossing at Berwick and continuing to the A27. Cross over and pass the English Wine Centre and Drusilla's on your left. Alfriston is a little over 1¼ miles. In the village watch for the Star Inn on your right and immediately afterwards dismount to **turn L** into the narrow footpath signed to the National Trust owned 'Old Clergy House'. The route is straight ahead but to visit the Clergy House and Alfriston church follow the signs as they veer away to the right.

At the bridge over the Cuckmere River the footpath becomes a bridleway and bike riding is possible. Cross the river to the road and the 17th century Great Meadow Barn faces you. **Turn R** to

reach a T-junction by Lullington Court.

For the shortened route: Turn L here towards Wilmington.

Otherwise: Turn R, signposted to Litlington. In a further ½ mile Litlington Tea Gardens and Nursery are on your left and the Plough and Harrow to the right. Ride for 2 miles along the lane with views on your right to the White Horse and Cradle Hill. Colourful paragliders may be seen drifting downwards.

At Exceat, consider a visit to the Visitor Centre (see Seven Sisters Country Park below) or Exceat Farmhouse for refreshment. Cross the A259 and go through the gate into Seven Sisters Country Park where the paved pathway snakes

Admiring the view near Alfriston

Upper Dicker

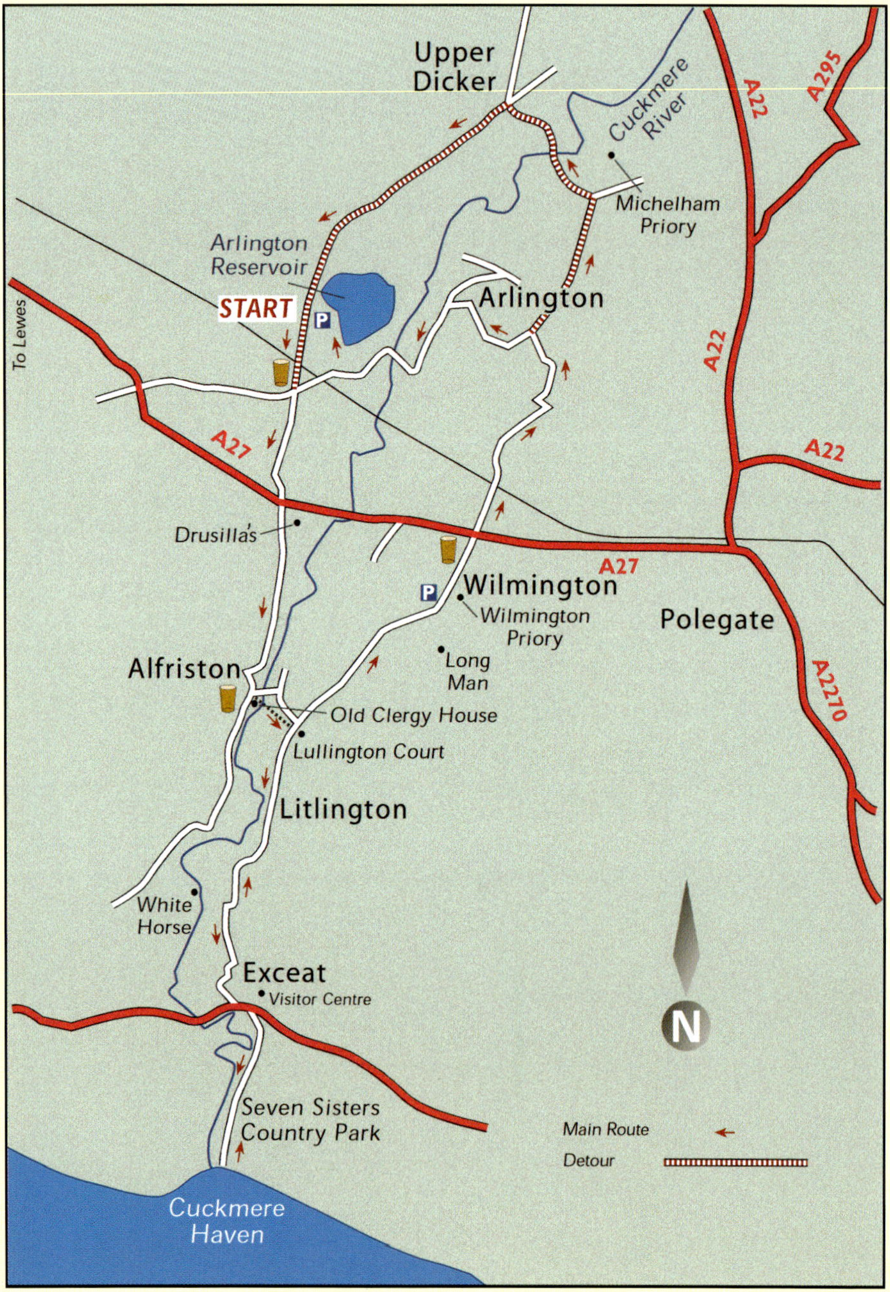

Cuckmere River

A22

A295

Michelham Priory

Arlington Reservoir

START

P

Arlington

A22

To Lewes

A27

A22

Drusilla's

Wilmington

P

Wilmington Priory

Polegate

Long Man

A27

Alfriston

Old Clergy House

Lullington Court

A2270

Litlington

White Horse

Exceat

Visitor Centre

N

Seven Sisters Country Park

Main Route

Detour

Cuckmere Haven

along the valley. This is an excursion of just over 1 mile past the spectacular meanders of the Cuckmere River to Cuckmere Haven. Follow the signs to the beach through gates on the final section. Return by the outward route to Exceat and on to Litlington.

Continue straight on in the direction of Wilmington. It is about a mile from the start of the hill to the top but you can take a breather by visiting the magical Lullington church, said to be the smallest in England. Push your bike along the narrow red brick path and soon follow the sign to the right past private gardens. Sit on a seat in the peaceful churchyard to gaze at the views.

Return to the route and, as you climb Chapel Hill, the panorama unfolds. Superb vistas continue for a further mile as you wind through the Downs towards Wilmington Priory and the Long Man, picked out in the chalk high on the hill. By the crossroads in Wilmington there is the welcoming Wishing Well Tea Rooms to the right and the Giant's Rest pub on your left. Cross straight over the A27 into Thornwell Road and ride for 1¾ miles.

Turn L to Arlington and **bear L** in the village opposite the Yew Tree Inn. After crossing the Cuckmere River continue for about ¼ mile.

Turn R into a surfaced drive and bridleway, identifiable by a South Eastern Water notice indicating the reservoir and Lakeside Farm. Follow the bridleway for ½ mile as it swings left past the farm and then returns to the drive. Just before reaching the road **turn R** into a grassy bridleway for a few yards to the reservoir and car park.

● ●

ALFRISTON
This is a picturesque village by the River Cuckmere. To the left of the main street and along a narrow lane, or 'twitten', are St Andrew's church and the thatched, National Trust owned, Clergy House by the village green, or 'Tye'. According to local mythology the stones to build the church were moved each night from the west side of the village back to the Tye. This, together with four oxen lying down on the Tye to form a cross, was considered to be a divine sign for the church to be built on this site.

SEVEN SISTERS COUNTRY PARK
The Seven Sisters are impressive chalk cliffs which undulate along the Heritage Coast from Cuckmere Haven to Beachy Head. The 700 acre Country Park is on their western edge where the River Cuckmere meanders through from Exceat to Cuckmere Haven. Cycling along the Valley Walk offers superb views of the river on its way to the peaceful and undeveloped estuary. Exceat is at the head of the Country Park with an Interpretation Centre, where there are exhibitions of the history of Cuckmere Haven depicting smuggling and many notable shipwrecks.

16

Hailsham, the Cuckoo Trail and Pevensey

13½, 18 or 25 miles

The Cuckoo Trail, designated for cyclists and walkers, offers smooth cycling away from traffic and tantalising glimpses of distant views. Ride to the Cinque Port of Pevensey where Roman legions landed and perhaps break your journey to stroll around the ancient castle. Then marvel as you meander along the lanes of the Pevensey Levels where sky meets marsh and meadow. A detour can be made to visit Herstmonceux Castle and the Science Centre on the site of the Royal Observatory. Relax at the end of the ride in the tea room at the Old Loom Mill. NB: Gates at the Old Loom Mill close at 5 pm.

Map: OS Landranger 199 Eastbourne & Hastings (GR 589073). 'Off the Cuckoo Trail, Circular Cycle Rides', is available from Tourist Information Centres.

Starting point: The Old Loom Mill, Mulbrooks Farm, Ersham Road, Hailsham on the B2104. Turn off the A27 between Polegate and Pevensey onto the B2104 in the direction of Hailsham and in about 3 miles the Old Loom Mill is on your left.

By train: Polegate Station is about ¼ mile from the route. Turn right out of the station and follow signs to the Cuckoo Trail. Ride along the Trail for a short distance to a junction and turn right into the route, NCN 21.

Refreshments: The Royal Oak and the Little Chef are in Pevensey. If you take the detour to Herstmonceux there is the tea room at Herstmonceux Castle and a café at the Science Centre. The Old Loom Mill has a tea room which closes at 4.30 pm.

The route: A comparatively level route on winding open lanes over the Pevensey Levels and on the well surfaced, off-road, Cuckoo Trail. It is a quiet route with the exception of nearly a mile on the A271 near Magham Down.
To shorten the route: At a signpost, prior to Hankham, **turn L** to Rickney on NCN 2 and join the main route. This saves 5½ miles and by-passes Pevensey.
To extend the route: Visit Herstmonceux Castle and add up to 7 miles to the main route. After the Levels **turn R** at the T-junction, signposted to Herstmonceux church and shortly **bear L** into a bridleway. At the road **turn L** and **L** again into the driveway for the Science Museum or for the Castle Gardens (entrance fees). Return by the same route.

Turn L into the Cuckoo Trail, NCN 2, and follow it for a mile over the Polegate bypass. At a junction of paths **bear L** into NCN 21, signposted to Eastbourne. (If you arrive at Polegate by train or park in Polegate you join the route here.) The path is lined with bluebells and celandines in spring and there are glimpses of distant views. In ½ mile **turn L**, signposted to Pevensey, NCN 2.

The way passes over the bypass and follows a quiet winding lane with views. Cross the B2104 and shortly **turn R**, NCN 2, signposted to Hankham, and continue for nearly 1 mile to a signpost.

To shorten the ride: Follow the route in the box above to Rickney.

Otherwise: Bear R, signposted to Hankham. **Turn L** in ½ mile, signposted to Westham, just before reaching the village school. Pass Hankham Hall, and ride over the A27. **Turn L** into Peelings Lane, signposted to Pevensey. Go past the village pond and **turn L** into the B2191, Pevensey High Street.

Cross over the road to St Mary's church, built by the Normans in 1080. Ride to the right of the green and then push your bike through the Roman west gate, into the castle grounds and along the footpath to the east gate. As there are seats this would be a pleasant place to picnic and perhaps explore the castle.

As you leave through the gate, the

On the Cuckoo Trail near Hailsham

Royal Oak pub is straight ahead and is a pleasant place to pause for refreshment, with a conservatory, garden and good food. The Old Mint House is opposite.

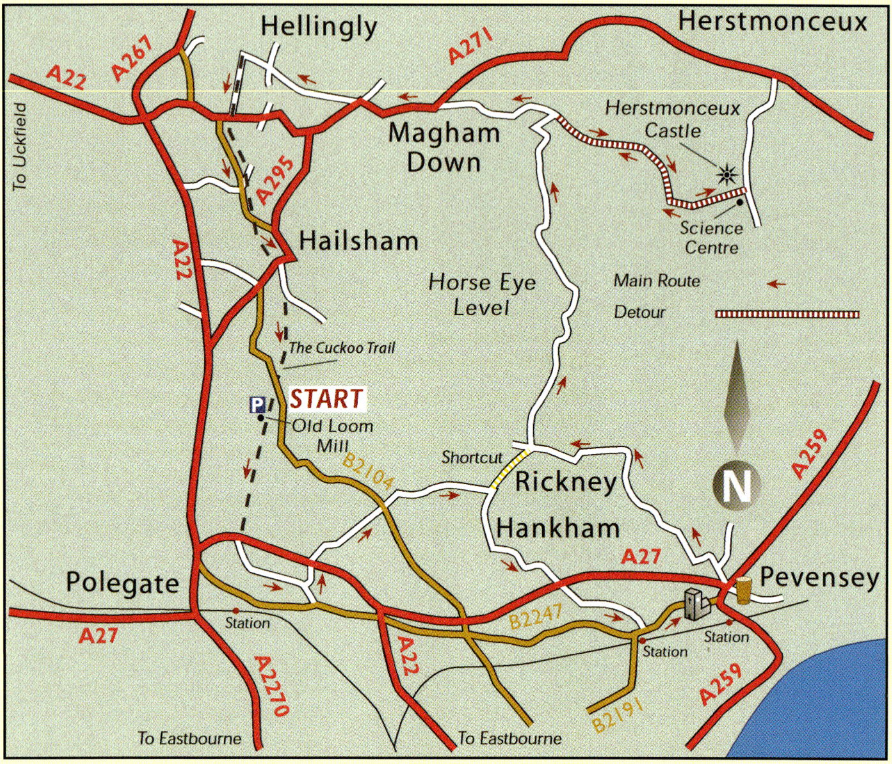

Facing the pub take Church Lane, which runs along the right hand side. **Turn L** at the T-junction, then **R** into the B2191, joining the A259 at the traffic lights. Follow this for the short distance to the large roundabout.

Take the second exit, signposted 'NCN 2'. Shortly **turn L** and continue for nearly 2½ miles in the direction of Rickney (the shortened route joins from the left). **Turn R** immediately after Rickney Farm, signposted to Herstmonceux, and follow the winding lane across the Pevensey Levels for nearly 3½ miles, passing Horse Eye Level on the way. This is a wonderfully peaceful area of wetland designated as a Site of Special Scientific Interest. In Roman times the sea covered the area but subsequently receded. There are drainage channels and cattle and sheep graze beyond the rushes that line the road. Climb a rise and panoramic views lie to the north where Herstmonceux church spire and the dome of the Observatory can be seen against the skyline. At the T-junction you have a choice.

The attractive Old Mint House at Pevensey

Either: Turn R to extend the route to Herstmonceux Castle and Observatory as detailed in the box above.

Or: Turn L, signposted to Magham Down, for the main route. Cycle along Under Road for just over 1 mile. At the junction **turn L** into the A271 through Magham Down and in less than a mile **turn R** into New Road in the direction of Hellingly. (Two roads fan out from the same spot. Take the second road, virtually straight ahead, ignoring the road to Cowbeech.) Ride up the gradually sloping hill for a mile.

Cross straight over at the crossroads and soon **turn L** into the path to the Cuckoo Trail, NCN 21, just before reaching the bridge,

and then **turn L** into the Trail itself.

Although the Cuckoo Trail is generally well waymarked with signs, these can be missed.

Bear L and go beneath Hawks Road bridge (ignore the path to Michelham). Where the Trail deviates into a housing estate **turn R. Turn L** at an NCN 21 sign on a wall by house number 38.

The Trail forks occasionally. Always choose the downward route as far as Hailsham car park. Ride anti-clockwise round the perimeter of the car park for 100 yards or so, and then **turn R** into Station Road. Pass a large pond on your left then **turn R** into Lindfield Drive and **immediately L** into Freshfield

77

Close. This in turn leads into a narrow path and the Cuckoo Trail.

From the edge of Hailsham the Old Loom Mill and its car park are about a mile down the Trail on your left.

● ●

THE CUCKOO TRAIL
The 17 kilometre trail follows part of the 19th century railway line that ran from Eridge to Polegate. It now provides a wildlife corridor from the High Weald, down the Cuckmere Valley towards the Pevensey Levels. The first cuckoo of spring was traditionally released up the line at Heathfield Fair so railway workers named the railway the Cuckoo Line. In 1965 the branch was closed by Dr Beeching. After nearly 30 years the Local Authorities and Sustrans became partners in the Cuckoo Trail project. The overgrown route was cleared and surfaced and now extends from Heathfield to Polegate. Watch for the original sculptures and hand-carved benches and also for wildlife. Birds such as the dunnock, which is grey-brown and similar to a sparrow, and the orange tip butterfly, which starts its life as a bright orange egg, are to be found in the area.

PEVENSEY CASTLE
The castle is managed by English Heritage, having been presented to the nation in 1925 by the Duke of

Devonshire. Tourist information suggests that you visit the castle and find out about its Roman origins, its turbulent history in the Dark Ages, its famous visitor 1066 and its role in World War II. It has a fascinating history and played a central role from Roman times to the Second World War. The massive perimeter walls were built in AD 340 by the Romans, and later the Saxons used it as a fortress. William the Conqueror established a headquarters there and the Count of Mortain, his half-brother, built a Norman castle within the perimeter walls. During the Second World War it was fortified and housed an observation and radio direction post. Telephone: 01323 762604 for opening hours.

HAILSHAM
E.V. Lucas wrote in 1903: 'the town exists principally in order that bullocks and sheep may change hands once a week. Hailsham's cattle market covers three acres and on market days the wayfarers in the streets need the agility of a picador.' It is now a busy and expanding market town with a good range of shops and cafés on a ridge above the Pevensey Levels. A Tudor mural found beneath the plasterwork of an ironmongers indicates that a few of the shops date back many centuries. In the 19th century it was famous as the 'string town' due to its rope and twine making industry. It even produced the specialised cord required by the Home Office for use by the official hangman.

Bexhill, Pevensey and Herstmonceux

19 miles

High Woods, protected woodland, is to the north-west of Bexhill, above Cooden. Ride down to Cooden and then follow the lane beside the beach with its views to Langney Point near Eastbourne before crossing the salt marshes where sheep and cattle graze. You may choose to detour and visit Pevensey and its castle, or the Old Mint House, before cycling along the marsh road across the Pevensey Levels. The Lamb pub in the village of Wartling is a good place to rest and offers home-made specialities. You can visit Herstmonceux Science Centre or the Castle Gardens (entrance fees), perhaps pause for a cream tea at Boreham Street and enjoy the wonderful tranquillity of the lanes on the return journey. Ride down Horse Walk Lane and cross Waller's Haven where fisherman try their luck, and you can gaze at distant views of the sea and experience the feeling of space that the open country offers in this area.

Map: OS Landranger 199 Eastbourne and Hastings (GR 715095).

Starting point: High Woods car park near Whydown. Take the A259 between Bexhill and Pevensey. At the roundabout at Little Common turn off northwards into Peartree Lane. At the crossroads go straight across and up the hill. The car park is about ¼ mile on the left.

By train: Cooden Beach and Norman's Bay stations are on the route.

Refreshments: The Star Inn is near Norman's Bay and the Royal Oak is at Pevensey. Wartling has the Lamb pub, Scolfe's Restaurant and Tea Rooms is in the village of Boreham Street and the Red Lion is at Hooe Common. There is also a café in the grounds of Herstmonceux Castle.

The route: It is virtually downhill or flat for the first 8 miles and then undulates. However, the uphills are neither very steep nor very long and good downhills follow. Generally it is a route of quiet lanes, although from the Pevensey roundabout to Herstmonceux there is some traffic.
To shorten the route: Turn R at Wartling immediately after the Lamb to save about 3 miles – but you will miss Herstmonceux and Boreham Street.
To extend the route: This ride can be linked with route 16 at Pevensey. Alternatively, follow the NCN route from Cooden into the centre of Bexhill to add 4 miles (return trip).

Turn **R** from High Woods car park and cycle straight ahead for 2 miles to Cooden Beach station. You will cross an intersection into Peartree Lane, cycle for a mile and then take the second exit at the roundabout, signposted to Cooden. **Turn R** immediately after the bridge into NCN route 2.

Ride by the beach and follow the road for about 4¼ miles to the roundabout. The road bends inland at the level crossing away from the sea and you ride through broad expanses of pastureland where sheep and cattle graze. The Star Inn, near Norman's Bay station, is on the far side of the bridge over the unusually named river, Waller's Haven. At the large Pevensey roundabout you have a choice.

To make a detour to Pevensey Castle and the Old Mint House: Turn **L** (first exit) and the Old Mint House and the castle are less than ½ mile away. You may choose to pause for refreshment at the Royal Oak. Afterwards rejoin the route at the roundabout by using the quieter Church Lane, which runs to the far side of the pub. **Turn L** at the T-junction and **R** to the roundabout to return to the route.

Otherwise: Take the third exit, the one after the A27 exit, and ride for nearly 3 miles to Wartling. You leave NCN 2 and ride over the Pevensey Levels along a road lined by tall rushes. There is a short climb to Wartling village and the Lamb pub.

The de la Warr Pavilion at Bexhill enjoys Grade I listing

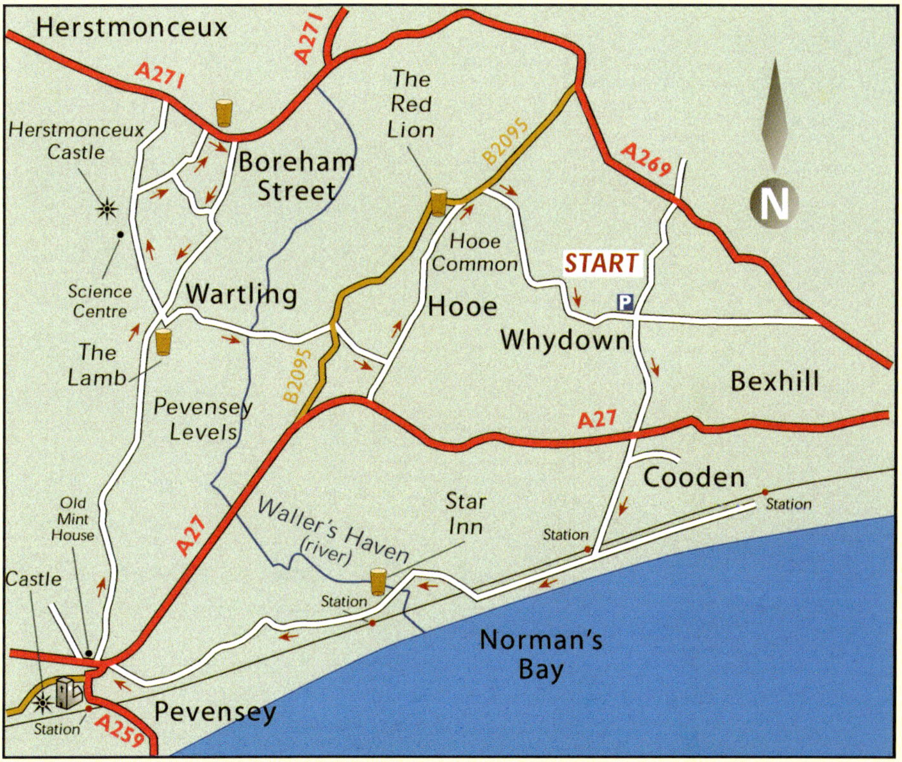

Map showing Herstmonceux, Boreham Street, Wartling, Hooe, Whydown, Bexhill, Cooden, Norman's Bay and Pevensey, with A271, A269, B2095, A27 and A259 roads marked. START point indicated near Hooe Common.

Continue for about ¾ mile and the Science Centre is on your left. Soon **turn R** into gently sloping Wood Lane to Boreham Street. **Turn R** onto the A269 for just over ¼ mile and Scolfe's Restaurant and Tea Rooms is on your left. Soon **turn R** into attractive Boreham Lane and ride for 1½ miles back to Wartling.

Turn L beside the Lamb pub and **bear L** as Horse Walk bends around. For 1½ miles enjoy a gem. Cycle down the hill and over the, now wide, Waller's Haven. Climb upwards between banks of stitchwort, bluebells and celandines in springtime. At the T-junction **turn L** and immediately **R** along Kiln Lane. In ½ mile **turn L** towards Hooe Common. Ride the undulations and in a further 1½ miles the Red Lion pub is on your left.

Turn R into the B2095 and soon **turn R** again, signposted to Bexhill. This is an attractive roller coaster of a lane for about 1¾ miles. Pass Whydown and at the crossroads of Peartree Lane and Turkey Road **turn L** to return to High Woods.

BEXHILL AND THE DE LA WARR PAVILION

Bexhill was previously a fishing village with a reputation for smuggling but it was developed as a resort in the late 19th

Make time to visit Pevensey Castle

century by the Earls de la Warr, lords of the manor. The gardens at Egerton Park were commissioned by the lords and the 1930s Pavilion on the sea front was named after them. It is now a Grade 1 listed building and is currently being refurbished with the aim of creating a major centre for contemporary art, architecture and live performance in the South East. Bexhill is promoted as a 'bit of quiet nostalgia' and little has changed since the 1950s. It has an award winning sand and pebble beach, so on a hot day why not bathe after your ride?

HERSTMONCEUX CASTLE
The moated castle, built in 1440, was one of the first brick-built buildings in England. Sir Roger Fiennes, of Norman ancestry, brought craftsmen skilled in brickmaking from Flanders, setting a trend for the building material of large English buildings. Sir Roger married into the de Herst Monceux family and the castle remained within the family for many years. In the 18th century it was owned by the eccentric Hares and fell into disrepair. The castle was restored in the 1930s by the architect W.H. Godfrey.

HERSTMONCEUX SCIENCE CENTRE
The Royal Greenwich Observatory was moved to Herstmonceux in 1945 to avoid the lights and pollution of London. It built up a reputation for world-class astronomical research whilst the castle was used as an international conference centre. You can still visit some of the giant telescopes on display, see the exhibits, investigate the Orbit Well in the Forces and Gravity Corridor or build your own bridge. Telephone: 01323 834457 for the castle and 01323 832731 for the Science Centre.

18

Robertsbridge, Bodiam and Battle

21 miles

Two wheels are an excellent way of exploring and sampling the treasures of 1066 Country. Robertsbridge has a wonderful collection of half-timbered and weather-boarded houses. The National Trust owned Bodiam Castle is, for many, the ideal of a late medieval moated castle and Battle is renowned for being built on the site of the Battle of Hastings. You may see a steam train on the Kent and East Sussex Railway from the tea room at Bodiam or be lured from the route for a wine-tasting at Sedlescombe Organic Vineyard. Pause to admire the panoramic view over the High Weald after the climb to Netherfield. There is the option to ride the additional 4½ mile round trip from Brightling to the delightful house that was once the home of Rudyard Kipling.

Map: OS Landranger 199 Eastbourne and Hastings (GR 738240).

Starting point: The car park in The Clappers, by the playground in Robertsbridge. Take the A21 Tunbridge Wells–Hastings road, turning off westwards at the Robertsbridge roundabout. Go into Northbridge Street and the car park is on the right just over the bridge as the road changes name.

By train: Robertsbridge and Bodiam stations are on the route whilst Battle station is very close to it. From Battle station turn right onto the A2100 and ride to the Battle roundabout to join the route.

Refreshments: There are plenty of refreshment opportunities on this route: Salehurst Halt Free House, the National Trust tea room at Bodiam Castle, the Cross Inn at Staplecross, the White Hart at Cripp's Corner and the Queen's Head and the Clock House Bistro at Sedlescombe, also many options in Battle. The Netherfield Arms is over halfway but is a good place to rest with a wonderful view from the car park. Jack Fuller's Pub east of Brightling is yet another possible resting place, and ideal if you choose to continue to Bateman's.

The route: Indisputably a hilly route but if you have a bike with a reasonable number of gears the gradients are such that it is not too demanding, especially if you take your time. The long downhill sweeps make for a particularly exhilarating ride. There will be some traffic on the secondary roads but the lanes are quiet. There is only one A road, the A2100, for about ½ mile at Battle.

To extend the route: Detour 2 miles (return) to Sedlescombe village at the bottom of Sedlescombe Hill. Cycle back up the hill as far as the churchyard and **turn L** into Stream Lane.

To visit Bateman's: Go straight over the crossroads at Jack Fuller's Pub and turn first left, first right and first left to Bateman's. Return by the same route to the pub (4½ return).

Turn **L** out of the car park and ride to the roundabout. Take the second exit, signposted to Salehurst. Shortly you reach the attractive hamlet of Salehurst with its pub and church built by the monks of Robertsbridge Abbey. Follow the lane as it dips and rises and in ¾ mile, at the T-junction, **turn L**, signposted to Bodiam. Oast houses and distant views can be seen.

Turn **R** in ¾ mile. You can enjoy an easy ride of 2½ miles as you cross the B2244. The road dips sharply to the River Rother, and Bodiam Castle is on your left. There is an entry fee for the castle itself but the tea room is open to all and from the terrace you may catch sight of a steam engine as it makes its way to Tenterden or the smart carriage drawn by two horses that ply to the station.

Go over the level crossing by Bodiam station and climb to Staplecross, 2 miles away. The hill into the village has a convenient seat where you can sit and admire the splendid views. **Turn R** into the B2165 and pass the Cross Inn.

In about a mile **turn L** at the T-junction, signposted to Hastings (ignore the crossroads by the White Hart). Sedlescombe Organic Vineyard is on your right and may be open for wine-tasting if you have time. Continue on towards Sedlescombe.

The detour to Sedlescombe village with its weather-boarded

The medieval moated castle at Bodiam

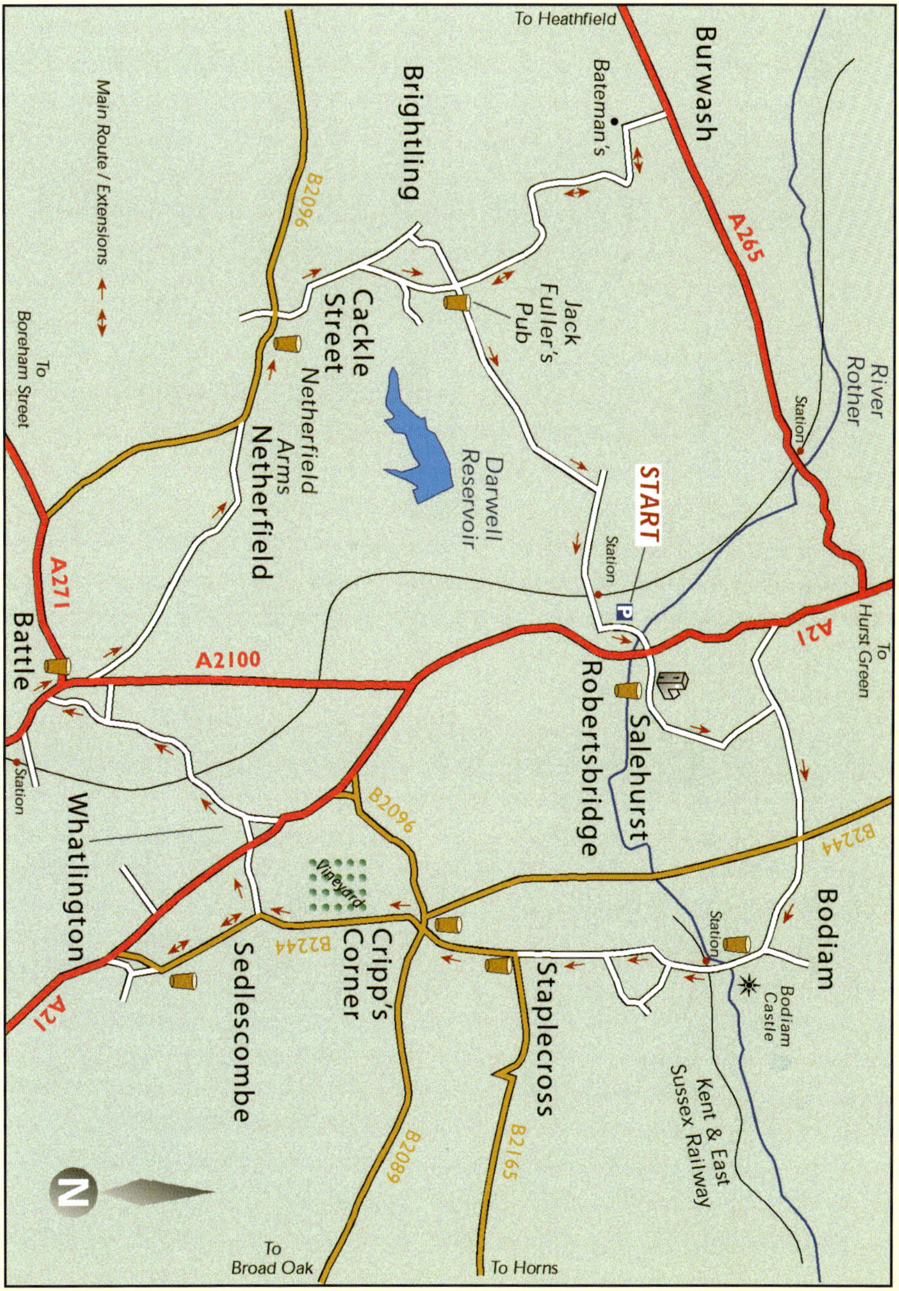

To Heathfield

Burwash

Bateman's

A265

Brightling

River Rother

B2096

Station

Jack Fuller's Pub

Cackle Street

Netherfield Arms

Netherfield

Netherfield

Darwell Reservoir

START

Station

To Boreham Street

Main Route / Extensions

A271

Station

A2100

Robertsbridge

Salehurst

A21

To Hurst Green

Battle

B2096

B2244

Station

Bodiam

Station

Bodiam Castle

Whatlington

Vineyard

Cripp's Corner

B2244

Staplecross

Kent & East Sussex Railway

A21

Sedlescombe

B2089

B2165

N

To Broad Oak

To Horns

Battle is well worth exploring

and Georgian houses set back from the long green is described in the box above.

Otherwise: Turn R on Sedlescombe Hill just before the sharp left hand bend and ride for over ½ mile along Stream Lane where wild garlic and bluebells line the road in spring. Cross the A21 into the lane ahead and soon **turn L** at a T-junction in the direction of Whatlington and Battle. Ride for 2 miles into Battle to the T-junction by the Olde King's Head.

In Battle, you may decide to visit the abbey, founded by William the Conqueror, on the site of the battle between the Saxons and the Normans in 1066. Whilst there, perhaps collect information from the Tourist Information Centre about other attractions in the town.

Turn R at the T-junction by the Olde King's Head into the A2100. At the roundabout take the third exit, the A2100, signposted to Sevenoaks. (Ignoring the first left hand turning) **turn L** by a brown sign to Netherfield Golf Club. Ride for nearly 3 miles, passing the golf course as you climb to Netherfield.

The Netherfield Arms is on your right just before a T-junction. This is a good place to pause and rest after the climb and you can admire the panoramic view. **Turn R** into the B2096, signposted to Heathfield, and pass the White Hart Inn. Sail down the hill for

1 mile and **turn R** at the lowest point, signposted to Brightling.

Pass Cackle Street and in 1¼ miles **turn R**, signposted to Robertsbridge. In less than ½ mile **turn L** downhill into a well-shaded lane, signposted to Robertsbridge, to reach Jack Fuller's Pub.

Either: Visit Bateman's, by using the directions in the box.

Or: Turn R to return to Robertsbridge, 2 miles distant.

In Robertsbridge **turn L** in the centre of the village and the car park is on your left.

● ●

BODIAM CASTLE
The castle stands in the valley of the River Rother close to the Kent border. Described by the National Trust as 'one of the most famous and evocative castles in Britain', it is a traditional castle with round towers, square gatehouse and ramparts reaching down to a moat. It was built in 1385 to guard the upper reaches of the Rother valley and the Kent Ditch following the burning of Rye and Winchelsea by the French. However, the castle saw no battles as the French

invasion did not materialise. The exterior is almost complete and there is enough of the interior left to offer a good idea of the life lived within its walls.

BATTLE
The town grew up on the site of the battle between William of Normandy and King Harold of England in 1066. William founded the Benedictine abbey of St Martin a few years after the Conquest and theories are that this was either because he had promised God that he would build it if he won or, alternatively, to atone for the slaughter. The high altar was placed on the spot where Harold was mortally wounded by an arrow. Later the town grew up by the abbey. You can visit the abbey ruins and the battlefield, where there is a signposted walk. At Battle Museum you can see, for example, a battleground battleaxe and engravings of the Bayeux Tapestry by Charles Stothard in the early 19th century.

BATEMAN'S
Bateman's is a Jacobean House, owned by the National Trust, which slopes down to the River Dudwell. Rudyard Kipling's home for 34 years, it was built for an ironmaster but Kipling moved there in 1902. He wrote a poem named *The Smuggler's Song* and it is said that he may have had the lawlessness of the local village in mind when he penned it.

Hastings Country Park, Winchelsea and Pett

12½ or 18½ miles

Hastings Country Park is a beautiful area offering superb views of the sea. Cycle along Pett Level, where you can climb the sea wall to visit the beach, and then make your way to the picturesque Cinque Port town of Winchelsea, high above the coastal plain and the sea. Go through one of the old town gates, now standing in solitude in the country, and enjoy wonderful views across the Levels from Wickham Rock Lane. In the village of Pett you may decide to rest at the Two Sawyers before climbing Peter James Lane back towards Fairlight. Here you can enjoy the panorama from a strategically placed seat and have a bird's eye view of part of the route you have cycled.

Map: OS Landranger 199 Eastbourne and Hastings and 189 Ashford and Romney Marsh (GR 860117).

Starting point: Hastings Country Park to the east of Hastings. Turn off the A259 Hastings–Rye road at Ore, about 1¼ miles from Hastings Old Town, taking the road to Fairlight. The Country Park car park is about 2 miles on the right, just before St Andrew's church. Directions assume that you park in the second car park.

By train: Winchelsea station is about 1 mile from the main route. It is on the route if you take the extended ride to Rye.

Refreshments: For excellent light meals and teas try the Coastguard Tea Rooms, signposted from the Country Park. Before climbing into Winchelsea there is the Bridge Inn and in the town the 15th century Tea Tree is on your left (closed on Tuesdays). There are two pubs in Pett, the Two Sawyers and the Old Forge Brewery. In Rye there are numerous options.

The route: The first part has a long downhill section where there is traffic. A quieter proposed NCN route from Fairlight to Pett is yet to be negotiated and the Visitor Centre at the Country Park would be able to advise as to whether this is operational. At Pett Level there is a long flat section, NCN 2. There are undulations, especially in the second half of the route, but Pett Lane is a delight to cycle. There is a short climb into Winchelsea and a substantial ¾ mile climb to Fairlight.
To extend the route to Rye: **Turn R** in the centre of Winchelsea by the New Inn and then **second L. Turn R** into the A259. At the right hand corner **turn L** and follow the lane past Winchelsea station to a T-junction. **Turn R** into Dumb Woman's Lane and keep straight ahead (away from the lane) to follow NCN 2 cycle path to Rye. Return to Winchelsea by the outward route (a detour of 6 miles).
To extend the route further: Link the ride with route 20 from Rye.

Go to the Visitor Centre at the Country Park and, keeping the Centre on your left and the bike racks to your right, push your bike the few yards to the lane.

Turn L into Coastguard Lane, passing the tea rooms, and **R** by the church to ride down Battery Hill. There is a good sweep down the hill until you ride some switchbacks down to Pett Level.

As you reach the sea wall the Smuggler pub is on your right. Continue along Pett Level for about 4 miles to a T-junction with the A259.

At the T-junction near Winchelsea **turn L** into the A259, signposted to Hastings, to cross the bridge. The Bridge Inn is on your right. Just past Strand House Guest House, **turn L** and climb the short, but steep, hill up to Winchelsea. The road bends sharply right and shortly the Tea Tree is on your left, where you may be tempted to try their acclaimed '24 carat carrot cake'.

Ride to the New Inn, passing St Thomas' church on your left.

Either: Take the extension to Rye by following the directions in the box above. **Or:** Follow the road as it bends sharply left. In ¼ mile, where the road bends, go straight ahead, signposted to Wickham Rock.

The route continues for 3¼ miles.

Sweeping views from Hastings Country Park

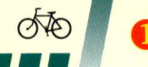

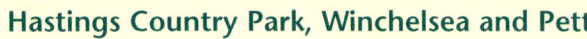

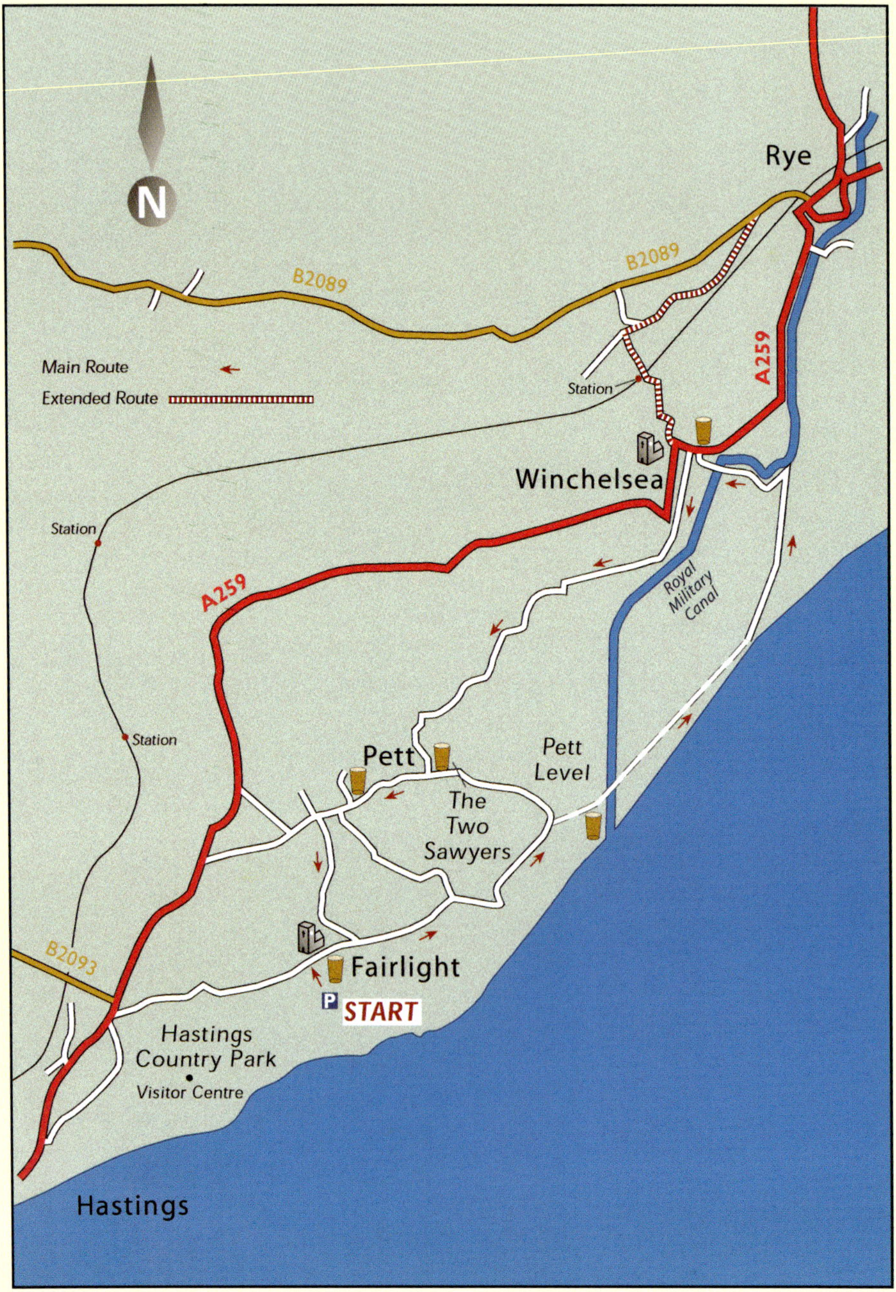
N
Rye
B2089
B2089
Main Route
Extended Route
Station
A259
Winchelsea
Station
A259
Royal Military Canal
Station
Pett
Pett Level
The Two Sawyers
B2093
Fairlight
START
Hastings Country Park
Visitor Centre
Hastings

You cycle through the solitary southern gateway to Winchelsea, 'New Gate'. The name of the lane changes to Pett Lane and just before this you will notice a windmill to the right, which you may have spotted from the Levels (ignore the right hand turn to Icklesham).

At the T-junction in Pett **turn R**. (The Two Sawyers pub is a short distance to the left and makes a very pleasant resting place.) Ride for just under 1 mile along the road, passing a church on your left and the Old Forge Brewery on the right. **Turn L** into Peter James Lane (second on the left after the brewery) and sail down the hill for nearly ½ mile before climbing ¾ mile to the top.

Turn R up the hill towards the Country Park for ¼ mile. There is a pavement if you prefer to push your bike. You can avoid a stretch on the road by pushing your bike up the few steps and through the gate into the churchyard. Richard D'Oyley Carte, founder of the Gilbert and Sullivan Opera, has a tomb here.

Leave the church and **bear L** into Coastguard Lane and **R** to the park.

● ●

HASTINGS COUNTRY PARK

The Country Park, much of which has been designated as a Site of Special Scientific Interest, covers 600 acres and offers spectacular views along its 3 miles of coastline. There is ancient woodland, heath and grassland, glens are filled with trees and there is prolific plantlife. The sandstone cliffs are suffering erosion but have some of the oldest rocks in the South East and are rich in fossils. Your passing visit by bicycle may inspire you to return to explore this fascinating area more fully on foot.

WINCHELSEA

Known as the smallest town in Britain, Winchelsea is an ancient Borough and still elects its own Mayor. Winchelsea supplied ships for the English fleet in the 13th century and was one of the Cinque Ports. The sea then retreated so that even the port on the River Brede could not be used, leaving the town high and dry, and the French wine trade was lost. St Thomas' church has only the choir and side chapels left whilst the stained glass windows tell the story of Winchelsea. If you see a black man in a red uniform in the churchyard you will not be the first, as village tradition has it that it is haunted by a ghost of this description.

20

Camber, the Marsh Churches, Appledore and Rye

26 or 32 miles

The ride starts on the magnificent sweep of Camber Sands near the well-preserved and picturesque medieval town of Rye, in the eastern extremity of Sussex. It then circles into the Walland Marsh in Kent where expanses of sky are emphasised by the Marsh plain. All but Rye is virtually at sea level. The road turns inland, away from the looming Military Ranges, towards the small but busy town of Lydd. Wind along halcyon lanes past grazing sheep and explore the fascinating churches of the Marsh. Attractive Appledore is just across the Royal Military Canal and here you will find antique and craft shops and excellent refreshment houses. Rye itself lies near the end of the ride. Consider parking your bike and allowing time to explore, browse and soak up the atmosphere in this unique town.

Map: OS Landranger 189 Ashford and Romney Marsh or Explorer 125 Romney Marsh, Rye and Winchelsea (GR 981182). To navigate your way through Rye a town street map is strongly recommended.

Starting point: There is free parking at Broomhill Sands. Take the A259 from Rye and, in a mile, turn right into Camber Road. Drive through Camber and the car park is on the right at its eastern end, about 5 miles from Rye.

By train: Rye station is close to the route.

Refreshments: At Camber try The Place, a relaxing brasserie with not only delicious food but also bike racks. In Appledore there are the Black Lion, the Swan and Bayleaves Tea Room. In Rye all conceivable refreshment options are available.

The route: This is a longer but easy route. It is on level surfaced roads or on gritted Sustrans paths. The Marsh lanes are quiet and the Military Road has little traffic, although what there is can be fast.

To extend the route: Winchelsea is less than 3 miles away. Use the Rye town map to reach Udimore Road. **Turn L** by West Undercliff and (ignoring the left hand path back to Rye) follow NCN 2 for 1½ miles along the track, through gates, to narrow Dumb Woman's Lane. **Turn L** into Winchelsea Lane and follow this over the level crossing by Winchelsea station. **Turn R** up the A259 and **turn L** into the town. Return by the same route.

The unusual belfry of Brookland church

From Broomhill Sands car park **turn R** towards Lydd, about 4 miles distant. Ride along the coastal road and near Jury's Gut Tidal Station follow NCN 2 as it goes into a track beside the road. On the outskirts of Lydd **bear L** onto the B2075 into Lydd town centre.

Opposite the church **turn L** into Denge Lane. In about a mile **turn L** again, signposted to Rye, into Midley Wall. This is signposted 'regional route 11' and follows the level area over Walland Marsh. In less than a mile **turn L**, signposted to Brookland.

In 2 miles, soon after a narrow crosslanes, **turn R** by a cottage at Hogstye Bridge and ride along this tiny lane, where convolvulus pushes through, to the T-junction opposite Brookland church. Push your bike through the gate into the churchyard and round to the front of the church. The unusual large bell tower is on the left.

Ride to the roundabout and using the crossing and pathway **turn L** into the second exit. Shortly **turn R** through the village and the quiet lane winds for less than a mile to a T-junction. **Turn R** and ride for ½ mile (ignoring the first turning on the right) to another T-junction.

Turn R, signposted to Appledore, and the village is 3 miles away. On the way you will see an isolated church on the marsh to your right. St Thomas Becket, Fairfield is the smallest church in Kent and was originally built in the 13th century entirely from wood.

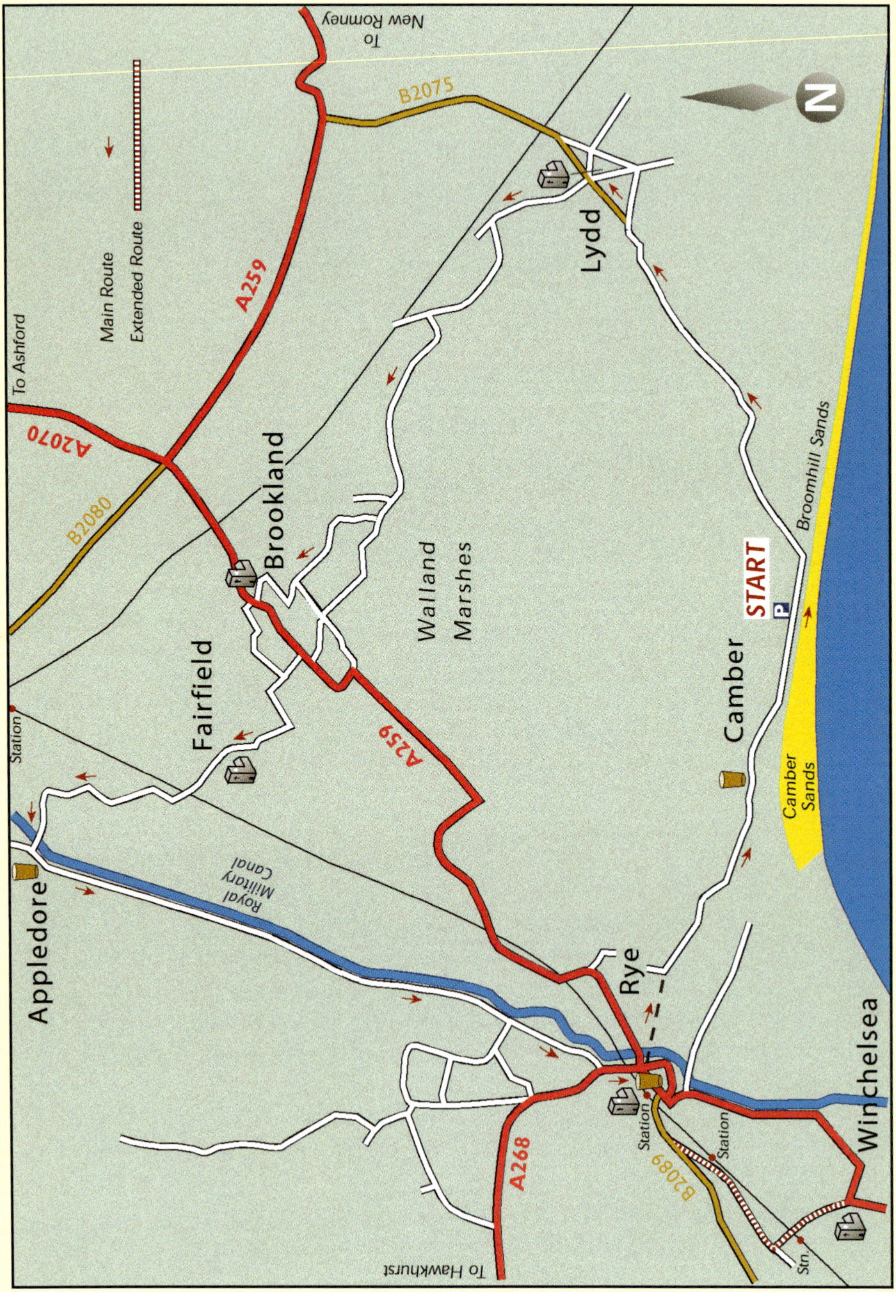

To New Romney

B2075

Lydd

N

A259

To Ashford

Main Route

Extended Route

A2070

B2080

Brookland

Broomhill Sands

START

P

Camber

Fairfield

Walland Marshes

A259

Camber Sands

Station

Royal Military Canal

Appledore

Rye

Winchelsea

Station

B2089

Station

A268

Stn.

To Hawkhurst

20 Camber, the Marsh Churches, Appledore and Rye

Stopping for an ice cream in Rye

Enter attractive Appledore by **turning L** over the Royal Military Canal and perhaps rest at one of the pubs or at the tea rooms. Return to the canal and **turn R** into the Military Road, which runs beside the Royal Military Canal for about 6 miles back to Rye. This is a long straight road. Watch for Tollgate Cottage on your left where the old toll tariff is displayed.

Either: Turn L at the T-junction into the A268 and cycle along the one-way system. At the roundabout **turn L** into the A259.

Or: To avoid the main roads, watch for a thatched cottage on the right. Just before this, and before North Salts, **turn L** into a short unmarked road towards garages. Push your bike along the footpath for ½ mile. You cross a railway line and emerge on the A259.

Shortly cross the A259 just before the bridge over the River Rother. **Turn R** into NCN route 2 and follow this to Camber Road. Cross over and **turn R**, still on NCN 2.

If you wish to visit the main part of the beach at Camber Sands, or find all day breakfast, **turn R** opposite The Place brasserie (3 miles from Rye) into Old Lydd Road and in ½ mile there is access to the beach on the right through the car park. The beach is safe for swimming but the tide comes in quickly.

Leaving the car park, **turn R** along sandy Sea Road and **R** again into Lydd Road. Camber Sands with its dunes stretches for 2 miles and at low tide the sea goes out for more than ½ mile. Broomhill car park is just after the end of Camber village on the right.

● ●

BROOKLAND AND THE MARSH CHURCHES

Brookland church is remarkable and particularly unusual because of its 75 foot detached belfry, which appears as something between three stacked candle snuffers and a pagoda. The marshy ground is probably the reason for the detached belfry as the heavy bells would have added to the weight upon the foundations. There are many anecdotes about this. One of these is that in the 12th century the master mason drew the body of the church and the steeple on two pieces of parchment. The tale goes that the builders misunderstood the drawings and thus built church and steeple separately. Lydd church lays claim to being the longest church in Kent and is known as the 'Cathedral of the Marshes'. Fairfield is built in an isolated position in the middle of pastureland where it used to be surrounded by a lake of floodwater. The Marshes are now well drained and most water is contained in dykes and channels.

RYE

The town rises above the levels to overlook the rolling countryside of East Sussex, Walland Marsh and the sea. It is a gem with picturesque timbered houses, the celebrated cobbled Mermaid Street, St Mary's church with its long clock pendulum, a museum, art galleries and treasures galore. In medieval times it stood on a promontory almost encircled by the sea and became one of the Cinque Ports granted special privileges for providing men and ships for the English fleet. Fish for the royal table was supplied by Rye fishermen. Rye declined in importance during the 15th century due to the silting up of the estuary, the recession of the sea and raids by the French, but the River Rother offers a waterway to the town and the fishing fleet survives to this day. The Tourist Information Office on the Quay offers details of the numerous places of interest in Rye.

WINCHELSEA

See route 19.